UNITAS
Leader's Guide

JOANN HEANEY-HUNTER, PH.D.

LOUIS H. PRIMAVERA, PH.D.

UNITAS

PREPARING FOR

SACRAMENTAL MARRIAGE

Leader's Guide

…er & Herder Book

PUBLISHING COMPANY • NEW YORK

The Crossroad Publishing Company
370 Lexington Avenue, New York, N.Y. 10017

Nihil obstat: Rev. Msgr. John J. Strynkowski, S.T.D.
              Censor delegatus
              March 24th, 1998

Imprimatur: ✟ John R. McGann, D.D.
              Bishop of Rockville Centre
              April 3rd, 1998

The following *Unitas* materials are now available
from The Crossroad Publishing Company,
370 Lexington Avenue, New York, N.Y. 10017:

Unitas Leader's Guide	ISBN: 0-8245-1755-5
Unitas Couple's Workbook	ISBN: 0-8245-1756-3
Unitas 1 set videotapes	ISBN: 0-8245-1757-1

Printed in the United States of America.

Library of Congress Cataloging-in-Publication Data

Hunter, Joann Heaney.
   Unitas : preparing for sacramental marriage : leader's guide /
Joann Heaney-Hunter, Louis H. Primavera.
      p.   cm.
   "A Herder & Herder book ."
   ISBN 0-8245-1755-5 (pbk. : v. 1)
    1. Marriage—Religious aspects—Catholic Church.
   I. Primavera, Louis. II. Title.

BX2250.H78 1998   98-22349
259 ' . 13—DC21   CIP

To our life partners and best friends,

Greg and Anne,

who have helped us to understand

the true meaning of marriage in love and faith.

Contents

Acknowledgments

Unitas would not have been possible without the help of many people. We thank the following for their time, talent, and financial support.

Special thanks to the following members of FADICA (Foundations and Donors Interested in Catholic Activities) for generously funding the development of *Unitas*: St. Marys Catholic Foundation; RASKOB Foundation; Frank J. Lewis Foundation; Trust Funds Incorporated; Komes Foundation; and one anonymous donor. We also thank Francis Butler, President of FADICA, for his invaluable advice and expertise.

We have found support and assitance from many members of the St. John's University community. Without their willingness to support the research and development of *Unitas*, this work would never have been possible. Thanks go to: Rev. Gerard Ettlinger and Rev. Jean-Pierre Ruiz, Chairs of the Department of Theology and Religious Studies; Dr. Willard Gingerich, Dean of the Graduate School of Arts and Sciences; Mr. Victor Ramos and the staff of the Office of Grants and Research; Ms. Leslie Bogen and Ms. Alicia DiBenedetto, graduate assistants for the project; staff members of the Offices of Printing and Reproduction Services; staff members of the Office of Travel Services; and Mrs. Lois Horan, for her assistance with the *Unitas* Conference.

The advisory board provided expert critique and support, especially during the early stages of this project. We gratefully acknowledge the assistance of Bishop Edmond Carmody, Diocese of Tyler, Texas; Dr. H. Richard McCord, Executive Director of the NCCB Secretariat for Marriage, Family, Laity, Women and Youth; Sr. Barbara Markey, Director of the Office of Family Ministry, Archdiocese of Omaha; and Rev. Gerard Ringenback, Pastor of St. Peter the Apostle Church, Islip Terrace, New York.

Two parishes, St. Peter the Apostle in Islip Terrace and Our Lady of Nazareth in Roanoke, Virginia, worked with us in the development stage of *Unitas*. The quality of this process was greatly enhanced by their wisdom, patience and energy. Special thanks go to Rev. Gerard Ringenback, Peggy and Richard Nixdorf, and the entire marriage formation team of St.

Peter the Apostle Church, and to Fr. Joseph Lehmann, Roberta Small, Fr. Kenneth Stofft, and the entire marriage formation team of Our Lady of Nazareth Church. In a special way, we thank Roberta Small for her work on several *Unitas* rituals, and Dan and Lynn Lonnquist for their work on the inquiry session. We have been blessed by the gifts of these wonderful people and will always treasure their friendship as well as their contributions to *Unitas*.

During the course of testing, we have had the privilege of working with outstanding people all across the United States. Marriage preparation teams from the parishes listed below assisted in testing *Unitas* rituals and sessions. In addition, we wish to thank the following parish and diocesan leaders: Mr. and Mrs. Butch and Linda Moses, Holy Family of Nazareth, Irving, Texas; Fr. Lowell Case, Our Lady of Perpetual Help, Washington, D.C.; Msgr. Joseph Bynon, Resurrection Ascencion, Rego Park, New York; Deacon James Healy and Fr. Brendan O'Sullivan, St. Anthony, Sacramento California; Fr. Joseph Genito, O.S.A., St. Augustine, Casselbury, Florida; Ms. Diana Gaillardetz, St. Cecelia, Houston, Texas; Fr. Mike Vetrano, St. Elizabeth, Melville, New York; Fr. Mel Hemann, St. Joseph, Rickardsville, Iowa; Deacon Ralph Imholte, St. Mary's, Colt's Neck, New Jersey; Fr. Roy Tvrdik, St. Mary Gate of Heaven, Ozone Park, New York; Fr. Phil Pryzbyla, St. Patrick's, Canonsburg, Pennsylvania; Fr. John McGratty, Sts. Peter and Paul, Manorville, New York; Mr. and Mrs. Wally and Winnie Honeywell, St. Pius, Houston, Texas; and Ms. Josie Curtis, Diocese of Beaumont, Texas.

The leadership of the Diocese of Rockville Centre, New York, has encouraged and supported the development of *Unitas*. Special thanks to Bishop John McGann for his continuing commitment to marriage and family, and Msgr. Frank Schneider, Chancellor, for his willingness to make marriage and family issues a priority in the diocese. You will always have a special place in our minds and hearts. We are grateful to Sr. Lauren Hanley of the Office of Pastoral Formation for working with us on the important task of marriage preparation training. Her insights and expertise contributed greatly to the development of our training efforts, and her friendship has been a source of constant support. We also thank Mr. Mike O'Leary, Ms. Rose Russo, and the staff at TeLIcare for their efforts in the development of the videotapes.

We gratefully acknowledge the efforts of Msgr. John Strynkowski of the Diocese of Brooklyn for his careful reading of *Unitas*. Thanks also to Fr. John Costello, Director of Family Ministry for the Diocese of Brooklyn for his support and willingness to make *Unitas* known throughout the Diocese.

We received expert post-production advice and assistance on the videotapes from Doug Fisher of Fisher Productions. His knowledge of theology and pastoral issues has helped us tremendously.

We thank Crossroad Publishing for their belief in *Unitas* and for their willingness to bring to publication this complex project. Our deepest gratitude goes to Lynn Schmitt Quinn, our editor throughout the project. She has been coach, cheerleader, unfailing professional, and good friend. She is any author's vision of what an editor should be. Without her careful eye, attention to detail, and willingness to work, *Unitas* would never have been completed.

In a special way, we would like to thank our parents, Joan and Tom Heaney, and Julie and Bert Primavera. Over the years, they have been our first teachers of love and faith. We thank them for the gift of life, and the gift of example that they have been for us.

Finally, our families are the source of *Unitas*. From them we have learned about who we are, about marriage, and about life. They have helped us to grow, to love, and to live. They have enabled us to reach far beyond ourselves. Each day, they actualize the phrase from *Les Miserables*, "To love another person is to see the face of God." We thank you, Greg, Beth and Kate, and Anne, Jim, Bill and Felissa, for helping *us* to see the face of God.

PART ONE

INTRODUCTION

CHAPTER 1

Parallels between the RCIA and Unitas

"The preparation of young people for marriage and family life is more necessary than ever in our times." These words of Pope John Paul II, taken from his 1981 encyclical *Familiaris Consortio,* present us with a challenge. How do we as a church provide outstanding marriage preparation for engaged couples? Pope John Paul gives us a direction for outstanding marriage preparation when he states that it should be "a journey of faith similar to the catechumenate." As many of you know, the catechumenate is a part of the Rite of Christian Initiation for Adults—The RCIA.[1] Through the RCIA, the Church welcomes people into parishes, educates them about what it means to be Catholic, and provides them with the support of caring, loving people who believe that living their faith is an extremely important task.

We believe that sacramental formation for marriage can best be accomplished by using the RCIA as a model. This is the starting point for *Unitas,* which is based on the four stages of the RCIA: (1) Inquiry; (2) Catechumenate; (3) Enlightenment; (4) *Mystagogia.*

- Inquiry takes place during the BEGINNINGS period.
- Catechumenate experience is provided during the Faith Formation process.
- Enlightenment is the Spiritual Preparation portion of *Unitas.*
- *Mystagogia,* or integration, occurs during the AFFIRMATION period.

Unitas emphasizes elements that are similar to those found in the RCIA:

- *Faith formation*—an essential ingredient for the journey toward sacramental marriage.
- *Information* to help couples succeed in marriage today.
- *Opportunities* for building connections with the local Church.

---

[1] Sometimes this is called OCIA, the Order of Christian Initiation for Adults.

We think that *Unitas* provides a unique way to address the issues of Christian marriage today in the midst of the local church community.

Inquiry/BEGINNINGS

In the RCIA, the inquiry stage serves to acquaint people who are thinking about becoming Catholic with the basic elements of Catholic tradition.

In *Unitas*, we call our inquiry period BEGINNINGS. It serves two important purposes:

1. It helps couples explore themselves and their relationship.

2. It helps couples learn more about the Catholic faith.

To accomplish these goals, we recommend one or both of the following:

1. A detailed couple inventory such as FOCCUS (Facilitating Open Couple Communication, Understanding and Study). This questionnaire can be purchased from the Archdiocese of Omaha, Nebraska.

2. A BEGINNINGS session such as the one instituted by Our Lady of Nazareth Parish in Roanoke, VA. See pp. 42–45.

In addition, some parishes add a Catechetical Session for some couples. See pp. 45–46.

Catechumenate/*Faith Formation*

In the RCIA, the catechumenate forms the center of the process. It is an extended period of time when candidates experience the Church in a number of ways:

1. They learn about the Catholic faith from Scripture and from Church tradition.

2. They experience church from the example of Christians in the community.

3. They celebrate the Catholic faith through the richness of the liturgy.

4. They encounter the meaning of their call to live faith on a daily basis.

In *Unitas,* we apply these steps to the formation of engaged couples:

1. They learn about sacramental married life through Scripture and Church tradition. They also learn to build skills for married life by using the best tools of contemporary behavioral science.

2. They experience marriage through the witness of marriage formation leaders and other members of the community. Married couples can serve as leaders and mentors for the engaged, and the entire community can support the engaged at liturgies and through prayer.

3. They celebrate at liturgies in their local communities. By participating in the rituals of *Unitas,* which ordinarily take place at Sunday Eucharist, couples will get a taste of loving, vibrant parish communities.

4. They encounter the call to live the vocation of Christian marriage each day. Marriage is not something that couples "get" on their wedding day; it is a lifetime of work and love together. Engaged couples experience this call through the married couples in the community, and serve as witnesses of love and faith to the entire community.

Enlightenment/Spiritual Preparation

The next stage of the RCIA is called "enlightenment." It is the time when those about to be initiated intensify their preparation through prayer and other spiritual activities. The enlightenment stage of the RCIA takes place during the season of Lent.

In *Unitas,* we recommend that the last two to three months before marriage serve as a time to intensify spiritual preparation for marriage. Couples have opportunities to:

- Prepare their wedding liturgies. They choose readings, prayers, and music for the celebration—in short, they begin to consider the spiritual dimensions of a wedding day.
- Prepare spiritually for married life by participating in activities such as:

    1. An evening or day of reflection for all engaged couples.
    2. A communal examination of conscience and celebration of reconciliation.

These and other activities provide the foundation for an enhanced spiritual awareness of married life itself.

Mystagogia/AFFIRMATION

The final stage of the RCIA is called *mystagogia*—the illumination period. This stage occurs immediately *after* initiation. It serves as a time when the newly baptized:

- Reflect on the sacraments they have received.
- Participate in the life of the community.
- Continue their education about the mysteries of faith.

This period is designed to help the newly baptized maintain connections with the Church community *after* the celebration of initiation takes place.

We believe that support of early marriage is a critical task of local church communities. While *Unitas* gives couples a good start, we need to provide additional resources to today's young married couples. We call our follow-up period AFFIRMATION. It serves as a time when newly married couples:

- Enhance the skills and faith that they have gained during *Unitas*.
- Grow as active members of faith communities.

By continuing to invite newly married couples to share in the life of the community, we are all enriched and blessed. On pages 141–143, you will see an outline for some suggested post-marriage sessions. We also have included a wonderful idea for a program of marriage enrichment from St. Anthony's Parish in Sacramento, California.

We believe that *Unitas* has many advantages over lecture-style marriage preparation programs or small discussion groups:

1. It emphasizes the spiritual values of Christian marriage.

2. It provides a Catholic context for couples who may not be acquainted with their own tradition, or who are entering interchurch or interfaith[2] marriages.

3. It encourages couples to become involved in the life of the local Church. Through the rituals of *Unitas,* couples are presented to the community as vital members who serve as witnesses of Christ's love for us.

4. It gives communities the opportunity to welcome the engaged into their midst.

---

[2] "Interchurch" marriages are the marriages of two Christians of different denominations, while "interfaith" marriages are those of Catholics and non-Christians.

5. It expands on the information offered by most marriage preparation programs—by providing additional knowledge and strategies crucial for marriage success in today's complex society.

While *Unitas* certainly is not the only way to prepare for marriage, we believe that it offers high quality marriage formation in a local Church setting. We hope that *Unitas* helps couples achieve a "deeper knowledge of the mystery of Christ and the Church, and the meaning of the grace and responsibility of Christian marriage." (Pope John Paul II, *Familiaris Consortio*, art. 66.)

CHAPTER 2

The Role of the Parish in Unitas

As we developed and tested *Unitas,* we found that certain types of parishes seem to embrace it readily. These are some characteristics of the parishes where *Unitas* has been most successful:

- **An open, welcoming community.** If a parish has a strong sense of community, it will be likely to see the value of having couples drawn into its life. In a parish with little or no experience of community, it may be difficult for engaged couples and married leadership to understand why and how marriage formation can and should involve the entire community.
- **The presence of a working RCIA process.** If a parish community comprehends why and how individuals are prepared for initiation through the RCIA, it should be able to see how that model might be applied to marriage formation. Just as individuals can be prepared for the sacraments of initiation through shared stories, loving sponsors, and joyful ritual celebrations, engaged couples can be prepared in the same way. Through a process of sharing, information gathering, and community prayer and ritual, couples can grow in their understanding of a marriage begun in faith and love. Communities that have experienced the power of the RCIA can help transmit the experience to couples planning on a celebration of marriage in faith.
- **Willingness to enter into a continuing process of team development and support.** In some parishes where we have worked, the marriage preparation team feels unappreciated, overworked, and burned out. In order to sustain a process such as *Unitas,* parishes and dioceses must be willing to offer supplemental training, nights of reflection, and social gatherings for married couples involved in marriage ministry.
- **Inclusion of new couples to expand the pool of marriage ministers.** Marriage ministers need not be the people who are involved in every other activity in the parish. We have found that couples who "do everything for the church" are likely to burn out fairly quickly. We recommend that you reach out to recruit some new people—they'll like the invitation, and you'll get different people involved in the community.

- **Willingness of the parish leadership to support this process.** *Unitas* is not a quick program of marriage preparation; it is a commitment to building marriages through formation and pastoral care. Pastoral staff and married leadership couples must recognize that *Unitas* takes time, effort, and commitment to be successful.

Parishes without all of these qualities, however, should not think that *Unitas* is impossible for them. While *Unitas* certainly will not create a community where there is none, it can help to enliven a community through teamwork, creativity, and parish involvement with engaged couples. When people in the parish begin to experience the commitment of engaged couples, married couples, and pastoral staff to an extended process of faith formation for marriage, it can help serve as a model for other areas of parish life.

CHAPTER 3

Leadership for Marriage Formation

Who are the leaders of *Unitas*? We think that *Unitas* works best with a team that consists of married couples and clergy fulfilling a variety of roles. While *Unitas* can be completed with a component missing, we believe that it is most effective when a marriage formation team is built. Below are the job descriptions for each ministry in the *Unitas* process.

Sponsor Couples

Just as the sponsor is a critical person in the RCIA process, so is the sponsor couple in *Unitas*. The most important role of the sponsor couple is to walk with an engaged couple on their journey toward sacramental marriage. Ideally, sponsor couples will be chosen from the community to assist couples as they prepare for sacramental marriage. Sponsor couples may be people that the engaged know, or they simply may be members of the community that wish to share in the important process of helping couples prepare for marriage. The marriages of sponsors certainly need not be perfect, but they should serve as models for the engaged.

Many parishes have reported to us that it is easy to find people who are ready and willing to serve as sponsors. Inviting couples to be sponsors provides an opportunity for them to participate in a significant ministry of the Church community, so it is a real privilege for them. We also have found that while some couples are reluctant to give presentations, they are more than willing to work one-on-one with the engaged, and are well suited to this type of ministry. The role of sponsor is an important one that should be highlighted.

Sponsor couples are involved in a number of ways. They usually:

- Attend *Unitas* sessions with the engaged couples and assume a mentoring role during small group discussions and couple conversations. They must be willing to share their experiences of marriage with the engaged, and they must be able to support couples as they journey toward marriage in faith. We have found that this model works best. Some parishes, however, state that this time commitment is too much to ask of their sponsors. If you do not think you can ask the sponsors to come to all sessions, have them come to the BEGINNINGS session (if you use it), the first and last content sessions, and all the rituals in church.

- Serve as a non-judgmental support for the engaged couple. As one young woman noted, "The sponsors have no agendas about us. They are simply there to help us."
- Attend all community rituals with the engaged.
- Assume responsibility for reminding engaged couples about events in the parish. They also can help couples by following up with them after they are married, if possible.
- Help answer the questions of engaged couples.
- Serve as models of faith for engaged couples.
- Help the engaged and newly married feel welcome in their parish community. In several parishes where we tested *Unitas*, sponsor couples were asked to contact the engaged on a weekly basis, so they continued to feel connected with the community between the sessions.
- Pray for the engaged couples during and after *Unitas*.

We have worked in communities where sponsors have developed strong bonds with the engaged and have continued their relationship long after *Unitas* was completed.

Some sponsor couples have been invited by their engaged couple to assume a special role at the marriage liturgy. What a gift to that sponsor couple!

In some parishes, sponsor couples also do other things, such as:

- Leading small group discussions and other exercises.
- Providing additional insights and information about various aspects of *Unitas*.
- Administering FOCCUS or another pre-marriage inventory.

Because the role of the sponsor requires a substantial commitment, we recommend that sponsors only assume responsibility for one couple a year.

We think that a solid group of sponsor couples services the core of the entire *Unitas* process. They should be recruited, trained, nurtured and supported. Building a group of sponsors takes time and effort, but it is well worth it.

Presenters

Effective marriage formation presenters are people who have experienced marriage, and who are working day in and day out to live a marriage in faith. While there is no such thing as a "perfect marriage," presenters should be happily married at the present time and willing to share themselves and their relationships (including their struggles).

Presenters have two kinds of expertise—the expertise of their marriage in faith, and the expertise that comes from training. Each couple should have some training about the theology and spirituality of marriage, and the basic skills needed for a successful marriage. Presenters also should be able to speak comfortably before a group.

Presenters usually perform these tasks:

- Give reflections on one or more topics in *Unitas* and participate in group discussions.
- Coordinate their efforts with those of other couples giving presentations.
- Coordinate their presentations with those of the parish staff member on the team.
- Take part in some preparation meetings prior to and during the process.

It is important for the presenters to be willing to share about their marriages. For example, how do they experience and celebrate faith in their homes? How do they communicate with their spouses and children? By sharing their own relationship stories, the engaged get to see a real marriage, with its joys and struggles. However, the married presenters must be careful *not* to become the main focus of the sessions. Their stories simply serve as illustrations of various topics.

Remember, the presentations are *not* lectures or classes. They are opportunities for sharing and reflection on the mystery of a marriage in faith. If you feel as if you are on a forced march, cut a few things from your remarks. A good rule of thumb is that the presenters should be talking no more than twenty minutes out of every hour.

Effective presenters also are crucial to the success of *Unitas*. Engaged couples will get to know them personally and will use their experiences as springboards for their own discussions. The attitude of the engaged toward the entire community can be influenced by the quality of the presenters.

Note. Some communities may choose to implement *Unitas* by overlapping the roles of the sponsors and the presenters. If you adapt it in this way, the process will include additional variety, because some information and stories will be shared by the presenters and some will be shared by the sponsor couples. The presenters meet and work with groups of engaged couples about specific content issues, while the sponsors work couple-to-couple with the engaged on other issues.

Prayer Ministers

Unitas is a process of sacramental formation, and at its root is faith—the faith of the couples and the faith of the community. We believe that prayer is an essential way of expressing our faith individually and in community. A prayer ministry for *Unitas,* therefore, is a visible sign of faith commitment and is an important part of the entire process.

Several test parishes have given us suggestions for creating a prayer ministry:

1. One parish has a "prayer coordinator" for *Unitas.* This person is responsible for providing the names of the engaged couples to members of the parish community, especially the elderly, shut-ins, or school children. These people actively participate in *Unitas* by praying for engaged couples.

2. One parish has organized a group that comes to church at the time of the *Unitas* sessions and prays for the engaged during the sessions. These people are a visible sign to the engaged that the community is praying for them.

3. In several parishes, the engaged are remembered during the General Intercessions while *Unitas* is going on. Each week, the engaged and others in the parish community are reminded about the importance of marriage formation for the couples and the community.

These are just a few suggestions. We hope that they provide a starting point for your prayer ministry.

Hospitality Ministers

In any community process, hospitality plays an important role. In *Unitas,* hospitality is particularly important. Studies have shown that many engaged couples are not strongly connected to their parish communities, and as a result, they may feel very uncomfortable coming to a formal church program. The hospitality minister can help welcome couples and relieve some of the anxiety that they might experience as they venture into unfamiliar territory. We have found that the engaged appreciate an organized, smoothly run session. It helps them to feel welcomed if they know that the community is prepared for the session. Furthermore, we believe that couples who feel welcomed will be more likely to continue participating in the life of the community.

Hospitality ministers usually do the following:

- Prepare the meeting space.
- Serve as greeters when the engaged couples come to sessions and to rituals in church.
- Perform administrative tasks such as registering couples, providing them with nametags, making sure they have their materials, etc.
- Set up refreshments.

In general, hospitality ministers can help provide a comfortable atmosphere for engaged couples, sponsor couples, presenters, and parish staff. This ministry can never be underestimated.

Parish Staff

The role of the parish staff is crucial to the success of *Unitas*. We firmly believe that a team of parish priests and married couples is most effective for the process. According to a 1995 Creighton University study entitled *Marriage Preparation in the Catholic Church: Getting it Right,* couples reported that the involvement of parish priests is a key element of a program's success. According to the Creighton Study, engaged couples like to see their parish priest taking an active role in marriage formation.

Unfortunately, due to personnel limits, priests or other parish staff members cannot always be involved in every marriage formation session. If this is the case, engaged couples meet with the priest or other staff member at an initial interview, at the *Unitas* rituals, and at some of the sessions. If engaged couples have concerns that cannot be addressed by the team couples, they should be referred to the priest or other staff member. If the priest or staff member can't answer the question or help resolve the situation, he or she should have resources to which to refer the couple for outside help.

Priests or other parish staff usually do the following:

- Meet with the engaged couple at an initial interview.
- Administer FOCCUS or other pre-marriage inventory.
- Preside at or serve in leadership roles at *Unitas* rituals.
- Serve as a team member at *Unitas* sessions.
- Serve as a resource if couples need additional assistance.

When priests or other parish staff participate in *Unitas* sessions they shouldn't be afraid to share their experiences of life, of family, of vocation with its ups and downs. Over the years, we have come to see that many couples have no experience of the clergy outside of the church building. Help them to see that parish staff are real people, with real concerns of their own. Also, let them see the lighter side of the staff member. It helps couples to relax a bit more.

When presenting couples work with parish staff members, there is sometimes a tendency to let the staff person do most of the talking, or to let the staff person handle the tough questions. We believe that all presentations should reflect the perspectives of the entire team—couples and parish staff together.

In the sessions where the staff member and the couples are presenting together, they should be equals in the presentation. Don't feel like the staff person has all the answers—the married couples have plenty of expertise to share.

Finally, we don't think it's effective to have a staff member give an entire presentation—in particular, the theology of marriage. Engaged couples must see that married presenters have something important to contribute to a theological discussion on marriage.

Community Members

As in all sacramental formation, the community should play an important role in the lives of the couples approaching sacramental marriage. The community's primary role is one of support for the couples. They support engaged couples through:

- Their presence and enthusiasm at liturgies where the engaged are present.
- Hospitality for the engaged and their families.
- Prayer for the engaged.

Just as the engaged provide an important witness of love to the entire community, the community witnesses faithfulness to the message of Christ and the Church by their presence at various liturgical events. Don't underestimate the importance of the community in *Unitas*.

A Note about Team Recruitment

There are several ways to recruit good marriage formation ministers. However, we believe that personal contact with the potential marriage ministers is the best way to recruit. Here are a variety of approaches:

1. A knowledgeable pastoral staff can identify couples who would be good role models for the engaged. These couples can be recruited by personal invitation.

2. Couples who already serve in *Unitas* leadership can invite friends to join them in this ministry.

3. If your parish has a ministry day or a ministry fair, you can recruit couples by speaking with them directly. Again, the personal contact with people who participate in the ministry may encourage others to join.

4. The experience of a commissioning ceremony for *Unitas* ministers or the celebration of rituals with the engaged may encourage volunteers from the community. People are attracted to a ministry when they think it makes a difference in the life of the parish.

5. In one parish where we tested, the pastor actively sought ministers from the ranks of those who were married 25 or 50 years. In the year of their jubilee celebration, they were invited to renew their own commitment by walking with a couple approaching marriage.

6. We believe that the least desirable way to recruit is to make a general announcement in a parish bulletin or at a Sunday Mass. What we have found is that this method does not yield good results. Many people hang back unless they receive a personal invitation.

A strong team can mean the difference between the success and failure of a process such as *Unitas*. The following are some advantages of a strong team:

1. Its members support each other, work with each other, and build the process together.

2. It has enough resources to prevent the burnout of individual members.

3. It enables people to discern their gifts to the community and helps them share their gifts with the community.

4. It allows its members to take a break when needed, without fear that the entire process will fall apart.

CHAPTER 4

Practical Information about Unitas

Any new process involves planning and attention to practical details. In this section, we have included strategies and suggestions from parishes that already have implemented *Unitas*. We hope that these suggestions make the process of beginning *Unitas* easier and smoother.

The Setting for Unitas

Unitas is primarily intended for use at a parish level. If you have a comfortable center that accommodates large and small groups of couples, conducting *Unitas* in the parish continually reinforces the connections between the engaged and the community.

In some parts of the United States, "in-home" programs have been the norm. The advantage of these programs is that small groups and a home environment may foster intimacy. We believe, however, that certain disadvantages outweigh the advantages:

1. If there is more than one small group of couples, the involvement of the parish staff may be minimal. This is a serious limitation when one considers that studies have shown the importance of both clergy and couple involvement in marriage preparation efforts.

2. If there is more than one small group of couples, and one or two married couples are presenting in their home(s), responsibility for *all* of the presentations falls on the leaders of each small group. This means that the married couples will be required to prepare all of the presentations instead of only one or two of them. For some parishes, this may not be a problem; for many parishes, it presents an insurmountable difficulty for and burden on the leadership.

Despite these disadvantages, some parishes may choose an in-home format for some or all of the *Unitas* sessions. If you have willing presenters and clergy, this can work, as long as the presenters continually reinforce the connection to the parish community.

While *Unitas* was designed with parishes in mind, we found that it can be adapted for use on a diocesan or regional level. Here are some suggestions for adapting *Unitas*:

1. Some dioceses prefer to hold content sessions in diocesan or regional centers. This may be preferable in dioceses that have small parishes and few weddings. In this case, the sessions may be held on a weekend, over a series of weeks, or on consecutive Saturdays or Sundays. All rituals and hospitality take place in the parishes of the engaged couples.

2. One diocese where we tested *Unitas* combined a weekend experience for the engaged with training for married leaders. To alleviate a backlog of engaged couples, the diocesan coordinator agreed to sponsor a *Unitas* weekend. Any parish that wished to send couples was required to do two things:

   • Conduct all rituals and hospitality for their engaged couples.
   • Send one married couple to the weekend so they could experience it and bring it back to their parish.

   The partnership between this diocese and its parishes reduced the marriage formation backlog in the diocese and increased the number of leadership couples for *Unitas*.

3. In some dioceses, there is an existing framework for one-to-one ministry to the engaged. In these places, the diocese and parish may collaborate by dividing content sessions between them. For example, the diocese could conduct four sessions and the parish ministers three. (How you divide the sessions is up to you.) Rituals and hospitality take place in the parish.

Flexibility and adaptability to a variety of situations make this an ideal process for diocesan and parish cooperation.

Unitas *Timetable*

As we tested *Unitas,* we discovered that there was some misunderstanding about its scope and time frame. Some people simply assumed that because it was based on the RCIA, it would take one year to complete. While it might be ideal to spread marriage formation over such a long period, we recognize that this is not practical for many couples today. In fact, some parishes repeat the program two or three times a year, according to the needs and ability of the engaged and the parish to come together in marriage preparation.

The *Unitas* timetable might follow a schedule such as this one:

1. Several months before starting *Unitas,* conduct a leadership discernment/training session so that people know what they are being asked to do when they volunteer to participate as leaders. You may do this on a local, regional, or diocesan level. At this session, you should:

   • Share job descriptions for each of the ministries. This will be very helpful for the discernment process of prospective volunteers.
   • Be sure to let people know the time commitment you are asking of them.
   • Ask people to commit to a specific level of participation (usually one year) and let them know that they can evaluate their commitment at the end of that time.

2. One month before *Unitas* begins, parish leadership should explain the process to the entire community. This can take the form of a verbal announcement or a written bulletin message.

3. Two weeks prior to the beginning of *Unitas,* parishes should involve the entire community in the *Commissioning of Marriage Formation Ministers* (presenters, sponsors, ministers of hospitality, ministers of prayer, and parish staff). (See p. 39.)

4. One month to two weeks before *Unitas* begins, hold the initial interview between the engaged couple and a parish staff member. This may include administration of **FOCCUS.**

5. **Week One** of *Unitas:* BEGINNINGS Session (see p. 42) or Session 1 (**Welcome** and "The Theology of Marriage").

6. **Week Two** of *Unitas:* Session 1 (**Welcome** and "The Theology of Marriage") and **Enrollment Celebration.** (See p. 48.) If your parish holds *Unitas* sessions on weekends, the enrollment celebration can take place immediately before or after Session 1.

7. **Week Three** of *Unitas:* Session 2 ("Communication Skills").

8. **Week Four** of *Unitas:* Session 3 ("Individual and Family of Origin").

9. **Week Five** of *Unitas:* Session 4 ("Values in Marriage") and *Prayer for Engaged Couples.* If there are couples who are seeking additional catechesis, start it here.

10. **Week Six** of *Unitas:* Session 5 ("Intimacy and Sexuality").

11. **Week Seven** of *Unitas:* Session 6 ("Balancing Practical Issues in Relationship").

12. **Week Eight** of *Unitas:* Session 7 ("Developing a Spirituality of Marriage") and **Closing Celebration** (see p. 53) with reception.

13. After the content sessions are over, you may choose to offer a **Liturgy Planning Session,** (see p. 55–58), **Natural Family Planning Workshop** (cf. p.111), or other activities for the engaged. (See pp. 55, 111).

14. Approximately six to nine months after your first *Unitas* series, is the best time to introduce the AFFIRMATION period (see p. 139) as a follow-up for the newly married.

As you can see, an actual *Unitas* series takes seven to ten weeks, depending on how you schedule rituals and other events. This does not include preliminary pieces such as leadership training, informing the parish, and the initial interview with the couple. The process of AFFIRMATION for newly married couples is an ongoing part of parish life.

We hope that *Unitas* can become an integral part of your parish and can enrich the entire community.

CHAPTER 5

☙

The Sessions

*U*nitas sessions are designed to be flexible and adaptable to the needs of individual parishes and dioceses. During the development and testing stages, we found that parishes and dioceses structured *Unitas* to meet their specific needs. For example, dioceses where Catholics are in a minority and weddings are few may present *Unitas* sessions in a central location to conserve resources and provide a better group experience for the couple. On the other hand, dioceses where thousands of weddings are celebrated each year may present all sessions and rituals in single parishes because the demand is so high. Rural areas may have different needs from urban areas.

Unitas sessions can be presented in a variety of ways, as long as the connection to the local parish is fostered and maintained. This connection is best made through meetings with the parish priest or other staff members, strong communication with local sponsors, and celebrations of the rituals in the midst of a welcoming community.

Time Frame

We have designed *Unitas* so that each session is limited to two hours of content, discussion, and activities, and each ritual activity is limited to approximately one hour. For the sake of all participants, engaged and married, begin and end each session and ritual promptly.

One parish suggested that you invite the group to gather together a little bit early for socializing. This way, the session itself can begin on time. For example: Gather the group at 7:30, allow 15 minutes to mingle, start the session promptly at 7:45, break at 8:45, resume at 9:00, and end promptly at 10:00. This will insure two hours of information and dialogue.

Prayer in Unitas

Begin and end every session with a brief prayer. This can take many forms—a reading from Scripture, a piece of music, shared reflection, the Lord's Prayer. We want to communicate to the engaged couples that we are creating a context of faith for the entire process. One goal of *Unitas* is to weave faith through everything we do.

In every session, we have included a sample selection from Scripture. These excerpts may be used as the prayer for the evening. They have been chosen from readings that are appropriate for wedding celebrations. We have used the NRSV (New Revised Standard Version) translation of the Bible for these selections. Couples, however, should check with their priest or deacon regarding the proper Scripture translation for liturgical use in their area.

We have also written brief closing prayers for each evening. Feel free to modify them to meet the needs of your community.

Working with Groups

Throughout *Unitas*, there are many opportunities for group discussion. In *Unitas*, group discussions usually are led by sponsor couples or presenters.

Sometimes group leaders are not sure about how to work with groups. We recommend this procedure:

1. Ask the first question and try to evaluate the sense of the group. A group may begin talking right away, but at the first session, it is very common for groups to start slowly, especially if the participants don't know each other.

2. Don't be afraid of silence. If the entire group is sitting silently for five or ten minutes, you should try to get the discussion moving by asking someone to respond or by giving your own input. However, you should not worry if there is a minute or two of silence while people are gathering their thoughts. Usually, someone will start talking, and once the first person starts, the rest becomes easy.

3. As leaders, you need to be aware of two types of people—those who say nothing and those who always jump in immediately.

   • Some people who say nothing may be bored and non-participative. However, many quiet people participate by observing and absorbing everything that goes on in a group. These people make important contributions if asked, but they may not feel the need to say something on every occasion. They should not be constantly pressured into talking. They have a right to their style and their way of participating in a group. Once in a while, try to draw them out, but don't force them.

- The people who never seem to run out of things to say present a different sort of challenge. While it may be easy to let them dominate the group, it is not helpful. There may be times when you must clearly state that someone else needs a chance to speak. You may also need to stop a constant talker on occasion. While these things may be difficult at first, you will get more comfortable with these skills as you practice leading a group.

4. It is often tempting to keep a group discussion going long beyond its allotted time. While this may be interesting or pleasant, it is usually not productive. If a group discussion is going overtime, invite the couples to come back to it at the break or at the end of the evening.

Couple Activities in Unitas

In developing and testing *Unitas,* we have found that couples appreciate some individual activities that are designed for them rather than for a group. Therefore, in most of the sessions, we have included at least one activity that is designated for couples. These are not designed to be group exercises; they are designed so that couples can share on issues that are specific to *them.*

In parishes where sponsor couples attend every session, we have found that the engaged couples like to discuss these issues privately with their sponsors. The sponsors offer support and another perspective on the issue. In this model, the individuals separate to complete their part of the exercise, and, when time is called, the engaged couples come together with their sponsors to complete the discussion.

If sponsors are not present at every session, simply have the couples return to the group at the end of the allotted time period.

Group Activities in Unitas

Even though couples want some time for themselves, most also indicate that they welcome the time spent discussing issues with other engaged couples. In almost every session, therefore, there is some group activity—usually a discussion topic or a role-playing exercise. The group activities provide a change of pace for the engaged couples, and they are usually very enjoyable. (Session 6, in particular, is definitely geared toward group discussion.) Group discussion gives everyone the opportunity to say what they think and to hear what insights everyone else has to share.

Role Playing in Unitas

Role playing is an interesting way of making points in various sessions. However, many engaged couples don't like the idea of being put on the spot to be the actors and actresses. In testing *Unitas,* we have found that the following procedure works well.

1. Ask if there is an engaged couple who is willing to take the roles of the couple in the scene. If you have an outgoing, talkative group, you will probably not have a problem getting someone to volunteer. Even if your group seems quiet, one couple might be very happy to participate in this way.

2. If you can't get an engaged couple to take the roles, designate a married couple to play the roles. This should be arranged beforehand so you are not scrambling for a volunteer.

3. If the entire group is uncomfortable with role playing, read the scene to the couples.

4. After the couple has completed the scene, (or you have read it aloud) ask the entire group to discuss ways of resolving the conflict. As a group, decide the best solutions, or state that many solutions could be correct, as long as they are agreeable to the couple. (This certainly is the case in the scene about where to go for the holidays.)

CHAPTER 6

Unitas *Materials*

The Leader's Guide

The Leader's Guide is designed to be a complete resource for *Unitas*. It includes introductory material, rituals and other activities, suggestions for implementing the process, outlines for all of the presentations, and a variety of couple and group activities (including alternative in-session activities that are not found in the couple books). One of the advantages of *Unitas* is that the process is flexible enough so that a team can design sessions around the needs of the couples in the group. Therefore, there is no expectation that teams will use every word or every exercise in the materials.

Leaders should prepare their presentations by focusing on the session objectives. This will give you a clear idea of what we consider to be the main points of every session. In preparing the presentations, carefully study the objectives for each session, and, in light of those objectives, decide which points you will present and which activities you will conduct. If you find that you need more exercises or content, you can always add them. If you need fewer activities and less content, feel free to cut out something.

There are some activities that are found only in the Leader's Guide. These include some in-session exercises such as group discussion questions or other activities that do not require writing in the couple books. The reason we have done this is so that leaders have maximum flexibility in choosing activities. There may be some activities where the leaders will be required to supply paper for the couples. As long as you are prepared in advance, this should not cause a problem in the sessions.

Group leaders should take a few minutes to go over the previous week's take-home activity near the beginning of every session. This gives the engaged couples an opportunity to ask a question or share an insight. We have also found that it gives the engaged the idea that these exercises are important.

Leaders should begin the session with these or similar questions:

1. **Did the activities raise any issues that you would like to discuss?**

2. **What did you like most about the activity?**

It is important, however, not to spend too much time reviewing the activity. The review should take no more than 7–10 minutes.

The leader's guide is the basic tool for *Unitas*. It provides parish staff and team leaders with the information they will need to begin the process.

The Couple's Workbook

The Couple's Workbook is designed to provide information about each session, and to make readily available all in-session written activities and activities for the week. Each couple receives one book, which includes enough materials for both partners.

Every activity reinforces elements of the sessions. Each activity sheet includes a discussion question, an exercise or some other activity that is specifically related to various session topics. In the Couple's Workbook you will find separate sheets for each participant, including extra blank sheets for writing exercises.

The Couple's Workbook also includes a copy of the Scripture selection for the week. Couples should be invited to pray together using the Scripture passage for the week.

As couples leave each session, they should be reminded that their at-home activity or activities will be reviewed the following week. Activities should be completed between sessions when the couples have time to think about them and to share their responses with each other.

Videotapes

Along with the written materials, you may have purchased a set of videotapes that communicate the content of each session. The videotapes consist of conversations between the authors, or between the authors and their family members. The videotapes correspond to individual *Unitas* sessions. They can be used in a variety of ways:

1. In some parishes, the tapes are used solely for married couples' training. Married couples preview the videotapes before preparing their presentations. They get a "feel" for the content of each session by watching and listening to the tapes.

2. In some parishes, videotapes are incorporated as part of one or more session presentations. To use the videotapes this way, the leaders should preview each tape with their session outlines. Determine where you want to start and stop each videotape and make a note in your outline. Cue the tape so that you begin at the right place.

- Each segment of videotape makes a few main points. For example, in Session 1, which presents the theology of marriage, the main points are:

  1. Marriage is a partnership and a treasure.
  2. Christian marriage consists of two individuals joining to form a couple in Christ.
  3. Engaged couples have specific hopes for marriage.
  4. Christian marriage is a symbol, sacrament and covenant.

- Show all or part of the segment, depending upon which points you wish to make. Stop and start the tape to suit your purposes. For example, if you only wish to use the videotape for the section on sacrament and covenant, set the tape at the proper spot in Session 1 and stop it when the desired information is presented.
- We have found that the taped segments require transitions from the group leaders. For example, in Session 1, we discuss the meanings of sign and symbol. The leaders should ask appropriate transition questions such as:

  1. **How do you think Joann and Lou understood the difference between "sign" and "symbol"?**
  2. **How do their statements fit in with the rest of what we've said today?**
  3. **How do their perspectives relate to your understanding of marriage?**

- You will note that sections of the tape correspond to the outline. For example, the second half of the Session 5 videotape clearly outlines the Church's teaching on sexuality. If you are using the videotape to substitute for a live presentation, simply eliminate that section from your own talk and proceed with the appropriate activities.

Note. We do not recommend that you substitute videotapes for live presentations at all or even most of the sessions. Instead, they should be used to enhance or supplement your presentations, or for variety. We believe it is very important for the engaged couples to hear your stories and examples, and to interact with you.

Evaluations

We believe that evaluation is a crucial element of any parish process. It is important to find out how people perceive the process, and how it can be improved for the future. At the end of *Unitas* please evaluate all sessions and rituals. There are standardized evaluations found at the end of the Leader's Guide and the Couple's Workbooks. The form in the Leader's Guide is for the team—presenters, sponsors, and parish staff. (See p. 135.) The engaged couple's evaluation forms are at the end of their Workbook.

Team members should copy their evaluation forms for each series of *Unitas*.

Many people are uneasy at the thought of being evaluated. However, remember that the input you receive from evaluations will help to make your next presentation of *Unitas* stronger and more helpful to those you serve—the engaged couples and the entire church community.

In evaluating *Unitas*, use the following procedure:

1. Ask each engaged person to complete an evaluation form and submit it to the team at the end of Session 7. Some parishes ask the couples to bring the completed evaluations with them to the closing celebration. This way, no time is taken out of the session. Remind the couples that their input is very significant, if *Unitas* is to be stronger in the future.

2. After all sessions and rituals have been completed, give every leadership person (sponsors, presenters, parish staff) a copy of the team evaluation.

3. Ask each person to complete the form individually.

4. Schedule a team evaluation meeting.

5. Discuss the engaged couples' evaluations, noting the way they perceive the strengths and the weaknesses of the process.

6. Discuss each item of the team evaluations, paying careful attention to the areas that the team found to be difficult or weak. Make sure that everyone gets a chance to give his or her input.

7. Try to figure out ways you can modify or strengthen the weak areas.

8. Use these evaluations as a tool to help plan your next series of *Unitas*.

We would like to hear from you. Feel free to contact us if you have suggestions or comments about *Unitas*. We can incorporate your ideas into our training efforts.

Other Materials

If you are using the videotapes, a VCR and TV monitor will be necessary.

A Bible is necessary for every session. We recommend *The New American Bible*, the *New Jerusalem Bible*, or the *New Revised Standard Version*. All of our Scripture selections have been taken from the *New Revised Standard Version*, and are used with permission.

It is helpful to have a tape or CD player on hand for appropriate music. A little music sometimes can create a nice atmosphere for the couples.

CHAPTER 7

A Note About Cohabiting Couples

(A word of thanks to Dr. James Healy, Director of the Center for Family Ministry in Joliet, Illinois. For further information, see his article, "Cohabitation: What Do We Know? What Do We Do?" Liguorian [October 1996] 4-10.)

Over the past few years, we have worked with many couples who live together before marriage. These couples, and the issues they face, cause concern for people who prepare them for marriage in the Church. Studies show that large numbers of couples live together before they marry, and some see cohabitation as an alternative to marriage. They also show that for a number of reasons, including less traditional values and doubts about permanent commitment, couples who live together before marriage are at a greater risk for divorce than couples who do not.

In working with cohabiting couples, we all struggle with questions such as: How do we address cohabitation with them? What do we expect them to do?

To answer these questions, it is important for you to be aware of some of the reasons why couples may live together before marriage. For example, some couples "slip into" cohabitation by staying overnight together more and more often. Others live together because they have seen so much divorce. They are afraid that they will not be able commit to marriage, so they "try it out" by cohabiting. Finally, some couples live together for economic reasons. They may live together if their culture demands an expensive wedding celebration, or they may simply assume that they will save money if they live together. While there are other reasons for living together, these examples represent some of the more common ones.

Just as there are a variety of reasons why couples live together, there are many reasons why they choose to get married. Some overcome their fears about marriage and make a commitment to it. This truly is a moment of grace. Some couples, however, have less than ideal motivations for getting married. For example, they may face an ultimatum: either get married or break up. If they are not willing to break up, they may drift into marriage. Since they have not made a free choice for marriage, they may be headed for trouble down the road. Others may see their relationship falling apart, so they get married in an effort to salvage it. Just as some married couples think that having a child will help a troubled marriage, some cohabiting couples think that getting married will save a troubled relationship. This strategy usually does not work.

Whatever their reasons for living together, the couples you work with have reached the point where they wish to be married. Your tasks are to help them understand the nature of the commitment they are making, and to help them appreciate the Catholic Church's values about sacramental marriage. The way you relate to them will certainly affect their view of the Church community and its teaching on marriage.

Some Pastoral Responses to Cohabitation

As a starting point, think about Pope John Paul II's document *Familiaris Consortio* (no. 81b). Although it is very clear that the pope does not support cohabitation, he recognizes that the entire Church community must reach out to these couples and help them see the importance of making a lifetime commitment to marriage. Instead of turning cohabiting couples away, we are called to get to know them, offer them pastoral care, and work with them in a caring, non-judgmental way. Cohabiting couples who come to the Church for marriage should be welcomed and encouraged for making this important step in faith.

We recommend that you keep in mind the following guidelines when you work with cohabiting couples:

1. Greet them warmly, and express appreciation that they have made the choice to marry. What they are doing by making this choice is actually counter-cultural and takes great courage.

2. Do not, however, ignore their cohabitation. As representatives of Church communities, you have a responsibility to teach the Church's views toward cohabitation. Keep in mind that helping couples work toward a sacramental marriage doesn't mean that you support their decision to live together. Instead, you support the step toward marriage that they are taking now.

3. Ask yourselves the questions: Are the couples with whom you work able to recognize the difference between living together and entering into a sacramental marriage? Are they ready to take the leap of faith that is required to live this new life together, transformed by their commitment and the grace of the sacrament? If they are, they are headed in the right direction.

4. Encourage the couples to deal with questions surrounding their cohabitation. Help them to understand that the issues that led them to live together before a total commitment may be the issues that contribute to a divorce in the future. Remind them how important it is to address these issues before marriage.

In short, cohabiting couples who come to the Church for marriage have made a significant step in faith as well as love. Welcome them, offer them pastoral care, and help them to understand the sanctity and the beauty of their marriage commitment made in faith.

CHAPTER 8

A Word of Encouragement

After testing *Unitas* in many parts of the country, we think that it is important to include this note. Any time that you embark on a new venture, there is a level of discomfort. We have found that this is also the case with *Unitas*. If there are couples in your parish who have been involved in other marriage preparation efforts, or who have served as leaders in various marriage movements, *Unitas* may be significantly different in style from those programs. Even though we cover many of the same topics, the primary focus of *Unitas* is to help couples experience sacramental marriage formation in the context of a vibrant church community. It is, by its nature, more communal, and where more people are involved, more coordination must take place.

We have found that early in the first presentation of *Unitas,* many married couples think that it is challenging. By the end of the first series, and certainly by the second time through, they find it to be much easier and much more comfortable. So take heart! Your perseverance will pay off.

Finally, remember that no matter what you do, you cannot *make* people believe or experience something. Just as the RCIA introduces people to an experience of Catholic Christianity, *Unitas* introduces couples to sacramental marriage in the context of a local church community. Your job is to plant seeds that may bear fruit now or at some later time. You may not *make* these couples "better Catholics," but you will help them experience your belief in God, in the Church community, and in them. Just leave the rest up to God!

PART TWO

RITUALS
AND OTHER
ACTIVITIES

CHAPTER 1

The Rituals and Activities of Unitas

As you already have seen, we believe that connecting couples to a parish community is a crucial part of *Unitas*. Regardless of how and where content sessions are presented, engaged couples should experience the celebrations and hospitality of their parish communities. By participating in these liturgical rituals and other activities, we hope that couples will:

- Experience what it means to belong to a loving community of faith.
- Understand the relationship between marriage and the church community.

We have designed a variety of rituals and activities to connect couples to their parishes. In this section of the leaders guide, we describe the following activities:

1. Commissioning of the *Unitas* team

2. "Inquiry" activities:

   - FOCCUS
   - BEGINNINGS Session
   - Catechetical Session

3. Enrollment Ritual for Engaged Couples

4. A Celebration of the Engaged Couples' Journey

5. Concluding Celebration for *Unitas*

6. Liturgy Planning Session.

First Things First

Before beginning a series of *Unitas,* it is important to prepare the community for what will take place with the engaged couples and the marriage ministers. The entire community must understand the importance of marriage for the Church, and the significance of the commitment that the engaged and leadership couples are making. The community should be aware of *Unitas* events, and should be encouraged to pray for the success of the process.

CHAPTER 2

⁂

Commissioning of the Marriage Formation Team

It is essential that the contributions of ministers be acknowledged and celebrated. Vibrant communities frequently celebrate the richness of talents found in their midst, and find ways to do that publicly. Certainly, when embarking on a process such as *Unitas*, it is important to publicly acknowledge the significant contributions of marriage formation ministers.

Married couples and individuals serve *Unitas* in a variety of ways:

- Sponsoring engaged couples.
- Giving presentations.
- Coordinating prayer for the engaged and the team.
- Offering hospitality.
- Assuming administrative responsibilities.
- Volunteering to provide child care for leadership couples.

We're sure you can add other things to this list. The marriage ministers are presented to the community as examples of service to others. We have found that great excitement is generated in the parish when the marriage formation team is recognized in a formal celebration. You may even get some additional recruits to help you.

Commissioning Celebration

(The commissioning celebration takes place at the Sunday Eucharist. This celebration originated at Our Lady of Nazareth Parish, Roanoke, Virginia. Special thanks to their marriage formation team for sharing it.)

After the homily, the presider or coordinator of marriage formation calls by name those to be commissioned. The marriage formation ministers should come from their seats, as a symbol that they are called from the community to serve it.

The marriage ministers stand in the sanctuary, facing the assembly.

Presider: My brothers and sisters, God has given married love a special significance in the history of salvation. You have generously agreed to minister to those preparing for marriage in this community.

So I ask you:

Do you commit yourselves to serve as models of faithfulness, love, and self-giving to the engaged in our community? **Response: We do.**

Do you commit yourselves to journey with these couples as they discern whether they are called to the vocation of marriage with each other? **Response: We do.**

Do you commit yourselves to pray for the engaged and all those who strive to live the married vocation? **Response: We do.**

Presider turns to the assembly and asks: Will this faith community support with your prayers the ministry of this marriage formation team and the engaged couples who will participate in *Unitas?* **Response: We will.**

Presider: Let us extend our hands and pray for these marriage formation ministers:

Lord God, you have made marriage a great symbol of your love for your people. Bestow on these, your servants, the fullness of your love and strengthen them as they begin this ministry. Grant them wisdom, understanding, joy, courage, and compassion as they serve the engaged through their words and example. May the Lord bring to fulfillment this good work begun in you!

Let us acknowledge our support for this ministry among us. (The entire community offers a gesture of support, such as applause).

CHAPTER 3

Inquiry/BEGINNINGS

In the RCIA, the inquiry serves as a time of evangelization. Individuals considering baptism are introduced to the message of Christianity, and are helped to discern whether they truly wish to become Christians.

In *Unitas,* or any marriage preparation program, most couples come to the Church already committed to getting married. How, then, does inquiry fit in? We believe that the inquiry is a time to begin the journey toward a marriage in faith, and to make a commitment to the process of marriage formation. We have outlined two ways that couples begin this journey. You may choose to use one or both of them—whatever is best for your community.

FOCCUS
(Facilitating Open Couple Communication, Understanding and Study)

For many engaged couples, the inquiry serves as a time to clarify issues about themselves and their relationship. While most couples know each other well, there still may be areas where conversation needs to take place. In particular, many couples need some assistance exploring themselves and the qualities that form their relationship.

We think couples can achieve this goal by:

- Completing an inventory such as FOCCUS. This inventory includes over 150 questions on a variety of personal and relationship issues. It can be used by pastors and marriage formation teams to identify potential difficulties in a relationship, or simply to get to know a couple better. FOCCUS, developed by a team headed by Sr. Barbara

Markey, Director of Family Life Ministries for the Archdiocese of Omaha, Nebraska, has been used worldwide for over ten years.[3] It is particularly helpful because it thoroughly addresses many issues of importance to Catholics, as well as the range of interpersonal topics found in secular instruments.

- Participating in a BEGINNINGS Session that introduces the couples to each other and to *Unitas*.

We recognize that some communities may be reluctant to add a separate inquiry session, such as BEGINNINGS. If your community chooses to use FOCCUS as part of the initial interview and does not wish to have a separate inquiry session, handle all of your introductions and housekeeping details in Session 1. If you use FOCCUS in conjunction with the inquiry session outlined below, simply modify Session 1 as described in the following paragraphs.

A BEGINNINGS *Session*

(This session was developed by the marriage formation team at Our Lady of Nazareth Parish in Roanoke, Virginia. Thanks to them for their insights and their input.)

First Hour: Getting Acquainted

Session Objectives

- To introduce the couples to each other.
- To begin the process of community building.
- To create a comfortable atmosphere for the process to begin.

Activity: Partners' Introductions

In order to set the tone for this activity, the *married couple* introduces each other first. Include in your introduction:

- Where you are from
- Family of origin background (how many children in family, etc.)
- School or work background
- Hobbies
- How you met
- How long you have known one another
- One meaningful experience that is a highlight of your relationship.

---

[3] Family Life Office, 3214 N. 60th St., Omaha, NE 68104.

Next, the engaged couples introduce themselves (or one partner may introduce the other), following the same procedure. The introductions should take no more than one minute each, or the session will never end. Even with one-minute introductions, this activity will take 45 minutes to one hour, depending on the size of the group.

Short Break

Second Hour: Journeying

Session Objectives

- To convey the idea that one's life is a journey.
- To demonstrate how marriage is a shared journey.
- To answer any questions about *Unitas*.
- To address any concerns of the engaged couples.

✍ Activity: Constructing an Individual Lifeline

1. Give each person one sheet of paper.

2. Ask each person to identify eight to ten significant experiences/events from his or her life and list them chronologically.

3. Give each person a piece of paper with a line drawn across the center of it.

4. Ask each person to plot his or her experiences or events *along the line*. Plot them chronologically along the line, from left to right.

5. Place positive experiences somewhere *above* the line, (the more positive the experience, the farther above the line you plot) place neutral experiences *on* the line, and negative experiences *below* the line (the more negative the experience is, the farther below the line you plot).

6. Connect the experiences with a line.

7. This individual work should take about 10 minutes.

Using page 44 as a guide, you could draw on a chalkboard or easel what a lifeline might look like. (You will notice that this is the lifeline of a married person.)

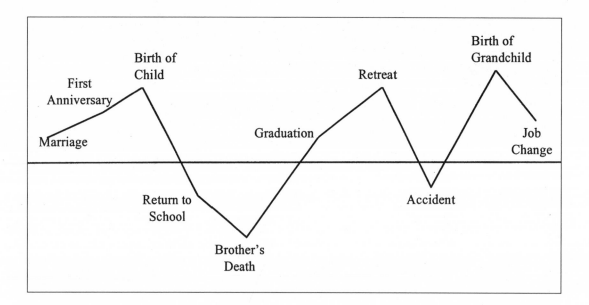

After the individual work is completed, each person shares the line with his or her partner. The couples should discuss their individual experiences, and observe the overall pattern of their line. Total time for this sharing will be about 15 minutes.

Group discussion of the lifeline: Invite couples to share their reactions to the activity for about 10 minutes. They should feel free, however, to speak or be quiet.

✍ **Activity: Questions about *Unitas***

The married couple can answer questions about the entire process.

Brief Introduction of Other Team Members

✍ **Activity: Introduction Ritual for Sponsors and Engaged Couples**

Introduction Ritual for Sponsors and Engaged Couples

The married leaders and/or the pastor go to the front of the room. They:

1. Remind the couples that they are at the *beginning of a process* in which they will reflect on two very important issues:

   • **Am I called to the vocation of marriage?**
   • **Am I called to the vocation of marriage with this person?**

2. Congratulate them on their commitment to *Unitas*.

3. Remind them that they are giving a gift to each other.

4. Tell them that they are a sign of love and commitment to the entire community.

5. Explain that, as they participate in *Unitas*, each engaged couple will have the support of a sponsor couple who will join them at each session, pray for them and maintain contact with them during and after the sessions as representatives of this community.

The leader calls each sponsor couple by name and asks if they will accompany the engaged couple in this process. As their names are called, each sponsor couple stands.

Leader: _____ and _____: as a sign of this community's support and care, will you walk with _____ and _____ as they continue their journey toward marriage?

Sponsors: We will. (The sponsors stand behind the engaged couple.)

When all the couples have been introduced, we suggest that they use the social time (which follows immediately) to meet each other and exchange phone numbers, etc. The social time helps people meet and mix.

Closing Prayer: Loving God, we give You thanks for the gift of these engaged couples who will soon be joined in marriage. We ask Your blessings on this marriage formation process. Help all the participants to be open to You as they journey through these weeks of formation. Be with us as we strive to enrich these couples as they journey toward marriage. Amen.

✍ Activity: Social Time

Conclude with refreshments and encourage couples to mingle for about 30 minutes.

A Catechetical Session

For some couples, further information about the Church may be necessary. We propose that these couples participate in an optional inquiry period that is similar to the RCIA. It is designed for individuals and couples whose faith background is minimal. It can also help interchurch or interfaith couples by providing information about the Catholic tradition. We recommend one- or two-hour sessions of questions and answers about the Catholic

Church. If an individual seeks more extensive faith formation, you should refer them to the parish's RCIA process.

In testing *Unitas*, we have found that many engaged couples who need extra catechesis are not comfortable asking for it or beginning it at the start of *Unitas*. We recommend that the catechetical session take place after Session 4—"Values and Conscience"—where we introduce the Church as a supportive faith community.

Possible Questions for a Catechetical Session

These are some topics that might be raised at a catechetical session. If you think others should be included, please feel free to do so.

1. What is the Creed? What are basic Catholic beliefs?

2. How do Catholics understand God?

3. What does "Trinity" mean?

4. Who is Jesus Christ?

5. What is the Church?

6. Why do Catholics say: "We are the Church"?

7. What is a sacrament?

8. Why do Catholics say that marriage is a sacrament?

CHAPTER 4

⁂

Ritual for the Enrollment of Engaged Couples into Unitas

The Rite of Enrollment in the RCIA celebrates and signifies a heightened period of preparation for the individual about to receive initiation sacraments.

The Rite of Enrollment in *Unitas* serves to highlight the role of engaged couples in the life of the community, and to welcome them to immediate preparation for sacramental marriage. Couples preparing for sacramental marriage are significant in the life of the community. Their relationships are symbols to the community of Christ's love and a challenge to all married couples to explore their own relationships in the context of faith.

In order to highlight the idea that marriage is not simply a "private affair," couples should be enrolled in *Unitas* in the same way that catechumens are called to election at the beginning of Lent. In this way, engaged couples clearly see that the community prays for them and supports them in their journey from engagement to marriage. In *Unitas*, the enrollment is combined with a special community prayer for engaged couples.

Enrolling the engaged at a celebration of the Eucharist is significant for two reasons:

1. The community has a special role to play in the lives of the engaged couples. Through participation in the enrollment, engaged couples have the opportunity to see a group of people who respect the commitment of engagement and marriage, who will support the engaged through prayer and hospitality, and who will offer themselves as models of faith and commitment to the engaged.

2. The engaged can have an impact on the community as well. Through public rituals such as enrollment, the entire community can experience the engaged as concrete witnesses of Christ's life expressed in human terms.

In our testing, we have found that the enrollment ritual highlights engagement and marriage for the entire faith community. We hope that it has a positive effect in your parish.

Some Strategies for Implementing the Enrollment Celebration

1. Before the celebration, the entire community should be prepared for the enrollment of engaged couples. Especially when *Unitas* is first introduced to the parish, the community should be helped to understand its importance, and the role of the entire community in helping couples to prepare for sacramental marriage.

2. The community should be encouraged to pray for the engaged.

3. Information about *Unitas*, and the names of the engaged couples preparing at any given time, should be included in the parish bulletin.

4. The parish should purchase a decorative book or loose-leaf binder that the engaged couples can sign and which can be displayed somewhere in the Church.

Enrollment Rite for Engaged Couples

Several weeks before a series of *Unitas*, the parish community should call forth its engaged couples for a formal enrollment into marriage formation. This underscores the importance of formation for sacramental marriage and reinforces the idea that marriage takes place within the context of the Christian community.

The ritual should be held in church, ideally celebrated at the Eucharist, after the homily. If, for any reason, the ritual takes place outside of the Eucharist, it should begin with a celebration of the Liturgy of the Word. Suitable readings and psalms may be chosen from the wedding lectionary.

Presentation of the Engaged

After the homily, the marriage formation coordinator should call individually, by name, the engaged couples and their sponsors. They should be called from their places as a symbol that they are coming from the community.

The coordinator states the following: These couples are beginning their immediate formation for marriage. They have been strengthened by their families, friends, and this community. After they have completed their formation, they will celebrate the Sacrament of Matrimony in this community.

The presider asks each couple by name: Do you wish to begin preparing for the Sacrament of Matrimony in this community?

Couples: We do.

The presider asks the sponsor couples: Sponsors, will you support these couples as they spiritually prepare for their marriages?

Sponsors: We will.

Presider: If you are ready to commit to the process of marriage formation in this community, please sign your name in the *Book of the Engaged*. While you are preparing for marriage, this book will be displayed in the Church so the entire community can pray for you.

A Prayer for Engaged Couples

Presider: God of life, today we humbly ask you to be with these couples as they continue their formation for marriage.

Help them to grow in respect, trust, and love for each other, so that they will be open to You as they prepare for this new life together.

Give them the wisdom and courage to look honestly at their relationship, so they can discern Your will for them.

May they grow closer to You as they grow closer to each other, and may they hear Your Word through the words and actions of the *Unitas* team members.

We make this prayer through Christ our Lord. **Amen.**

CHAPTER 5

A Celebration of the
Engaged Couples' Journey

In the RCIA, the "scrutinies" are rituals intended to strengthen the catechumens so that they remain united with Christ as they move toward initiation. (No. 154, RICA).

After three or four weeks of *Unitas*, the community celebrates a "scrutiny" of sorts with the couples preparing for marriage. In this ritual, couples are invited to the church to celebrate with the community and to pray for strength as they continue their journey toward the vocation of Christian marriage.

For engaged couples, this celebration can serve to focus attention on the spiritual dimensions of marriage and to help them grow as symbols of the love of Christ in the Christian community.

The Celebration

The engaged enter the Church with the ministers of the Eucharist and sit in a place reserved for them.

After the homily, the engaged and their sponsors should be called from their places to the front of the community. The presider invites everyone to spend a few moments in silent prayer. At this time, sponsors should place their hands on the engaged couples' shoulders.

Presider: Our community confidently witnesses these couples' plans for sacramental marriage. They are in the midst of *Unitas*, a formation process that will lead them to the beginning of their lifelong journey as a Christian couple and family. Let us pray that they will be ready to take this important step in faith.

That these couples may keep the word of God in their hearts and learn to understand it more deeply, let us pray to the Lord:

Response: Lord, hear our prayer.

That they may focus on Christ as the center of their marriage in faith, let us pray to the Lord.

Response: Lord, hear our prayer.

That they may humbly acknowledge the times they have hurt each other and be willing to ask for forgiveness, let us pray to the Lord.

Response: Lord, hear our prayer.

That the Holy Spirit may strengthen their commitment to each other and to God, let us pray to the Lord.

Response: Lord, hear our prayer.

That they and their families may put their hope in Christ and receive his peace, let us pray to the Lord.

Response: Lord, hear our prayer.

Presider: Couples, do you intend to marry in the Catholic Church, and live as symbols of God's love in the world?

Couples: We do.

Presider: Will you accept the support of this community as we help you to prepare for Christian marriage?

Couples: We will.

Presider to the community: Will you continue to offer your support and prayers to these couples as they continue their formation for marriage?

Community: We will.

A Prayer for the Engaged

Presider: God, the source of life and love, bless these couples as they continue their formation for Christian marriage. Strengthen their commitment as they continue to prepare for this holy way of life, and help them to focus on the true meaning of their life together. We make this prayer through Christ our Lord.

Response: Amen.

CHAPTER 6

Concluding Celebration for Unitas

The concluding celebration should take place at a Sunday Eucharist, to remind the couples of their role in the Church community. This ritual also reminds the entire community about the significance of Christian marriage, and about the witness of faith that the engaged can provide.

In our testing phase we found that parishes handle this celebration in a variety of ways. Many parishes have the celebration at the main liturgy of the parish. One parish, however, celebrated rituals at all the parish Masses. (For example, the Enrollment took place at the 10:30 A.M.. liturgy, the second celebration took place at 12:00 noon, and the Concluding Celebration took place at 5:00 P.M. on Saturday evening.) In this way the entire parish participated with the engaged at one point or another. One pastor, who served three parishes and conducted *Unitas* on a regional level, held one celebration in each parish. In that way, every parish met the engaged couples.

Suggestions for the Celebration

1. Engaged couples may process into church with the ministers of the Eucharist.

2. Perhaps, if one of the engaged is experienced, he or she can serve as a lector.

3. Many parishes give couples a gift at this time.

4. The engaged may serve as ushers, or present the bread and wine to the presider.

5. A reception for family, friends, and the entire community can follow the celebration of the Eucharist.

A Community Prayer for the Engaged

After the homily, couples are called from the community and presented to the community. The entire community offers this prayer for the couples.

Creator God,

We praise You and we bless You. In the beginning, You made man and woman to be partners in love and life. Be with these couples, as they continue their journey toward marriage in Your name.

Help them to be true to each other in the good times and bad times of their lives. Bless their love, and strengthen their commitment.

May they always know that You are the source of all that is good in their lives. We make this prayer through Christ our Lord. **Amen.**

SESSION 7

Liturgy Planning Session

We have found that a piece of marriage preparation often not emphasized by the couples is wedding day liturgy planning. While most couples invest many hours in planning the reception, they sometimes forget that the liturgy makes a statement about their love, commitment, values, and perspectives on marriage. By offering a session such as this, you give couples the opportunity to reflect on the meaning of their wedding liturgy. We recommend that it take place at designated times throughout the year (usually two or three times, depending on the number of weddings in the parish). We recommend this session, but do not think you should require it of the couples.

Some Strategies for Implementing the Session

1. Some parishes invite parents to this session. This may ease difficulties that could arise as couples are planning a ceremony that might be different from that of the parents'.

2. Some parishes also include a "music showcase" where the music minister plays liturgically appropriate wedding music.

The Session

The starting point for this session is the Catholic wedding ceremony. It is important to recognize, however, that many couples today are interchurch, intercultural, or interfaith. Special care must be taken to emphasize that these couples can have a meaningful religious wedding ceremony that respects their spiritual diversity, and highlights the common elements of the two faith traditions.

Elements of the Catholic Wedding

1. According to the Church, the ideal way to celebrate the sacrament of Christian marriage is at a special celebration of the Eucharist called a Nuptial Mass. At the Nuptial Mass, the couple exchanges wedding vows in the context of the celebration that nourishes and supports their faith.

2. A Nuptial Mass is very similar to a regular Sunday Eucharistic celebration, but adds special features to emphasize the importance of marriage, the newly married couple, and the family and friends of the bride and the groom.

3. **Procession.** At a regular Sunday liturgy, the procession includes the ministers of the Eucharist. At a Nuptial Mass, the procession includes the wedding attendants, the bride and groom, one or more parents, and the ministers of the Eucharist. Usually the procession is accompanied by suitable music. Couples should be encouraged to think about who belongs in the procession. This is not simply a showcase for the bride and her attendants; it is the beginning of the celebration of the Eucharist.

4. **Liturgy of the Word.** The Liturgy of the Word consists of the readings chosen for the celebration. In general, three or four selections *from the Bible* are used. The Liturgy of the Word is not the time to be reading love poetry. Normally, couples choose a reading from Hebrew Scripture (also called the Old Testament), a psalm (which is also taken from the Hebrew Scripture and is sung), a reading from one of Paul's letters or one of the other New Testament epistles, and a Gospel (from the New Testament—Matthew, Mark, Luke or John). Spell it out—you would be amazed at how many people think that Paul wrote one of the four Gospels, or that Jesus is mentioned in the Book of Genesis. Encourage the couples to choose readings in consultation with the priest or deacon who is witnessing their marriage

   The Liturgy of the Word is a place where family or close friends may be able to join in your liturgical celebration. It is important, however, to choose readers who can effectively proclaim God's word. If a person cannot read well, or will be very nervous—try someone else! When preparing readers, please make sure that they know where the reading will be, and how to adjust a microphone. *Under no circumstances should someone pull a piece of paper out of his or her pocket to proclaim the reading!* (This detracts from the presentation of the reading.) If a person is afraid that he or she will not be able to find the passage, it should be clipped into the lectionary before the liturgy.

5. **Exchange of Vows.** This is a unique feature of a Nuptial Mass. Emphasize that the priest or deacon does not marry the couple—the couple ministers the sacrament to each other. The priest or deacon is the official witness of the Church for the sacra-

ment of marriage. Encourage couples to check with their priest or deacon about the wording of vows. Usually, the vows take a very specific form. They must be unconditional and promise permanent fidelity. "As long as we both shall love" does not reflect the permanence of the Christian marriage commitment. Some parishes do not permit any deviation from the standard form—so check before you tell the couples anything.

6. **Blessing of rings.** Today, the usual custom is a double ring ceremony. Couples should make sure that both rings are easily accessible.

7. **Additional Symbols.** Couples sometimes wish to light a "unity candle" after the exchange of rings. Remind the couples that the lighting of a candle is not a primary symbol, it is an extra. *They* are the most important symbol of the unity that takes place in marriage. Be sure to check with the parish staff before you recommend any additional ceremony such as a candle lighting.

8. **General Intercessions (Prayers of the Faithful).** These prayers are part of every celebration of the Eucharist. At a Nuptial Mass, they provide an opportunity for couples to articulate their intentions for and with the entire community. They should usually follow this sequence:

   • Prayers for the church and world;
   • Prayers that focus on the general needs of the gathered assembly;
   • Prayers for the newly married couple.

   The prayers of the faithful are not meant to be another homily—they are simply intentions of the Church and the couple. They also provide another opportunity for family members or friends to be involved. Some engaged couples invite their sponsor couples to proclaim the prayers of the faithful.

   As with the Scripture readings, it is not acceptable to reach into a pocket and pull out a piece of paper with prayers on it. The person reading the prayers of the faithful should be prepared, and should have them ready and in the proper place.

9. **Liturgy of the Eucharist.** Couples should check with the priest or deacon about various options for the prayers to be said at this time. Couples may find that one version or another fits with their liturgical theme. Again, encourage couples to consult with their priest or deacon before they choose any prayers.

10. **Presentation of the Gifts.** This is a wonderful opportunity for grandparents, godparents, sponsors, and other special people to participate in the celebration. Participants in this procession don't have to say anything—they simply carry forward the gifts of bread and wine. This might also be a place where children can participate.

11. **Nuptial Blessing.** Couples should read the nuptial blessings carefully, and choose one in consultation with the priest or deacon. Some couples may not even be aware that there are differences in the nuptial blessings. Point them out.

12. Remind couples that at weddings, communion usually is given in the forms of bread and wine. Eucharistic ministers may be needed. (Family members, friends, and members of the parish community may be able to participate here.) A reminder: some families may not be familiar with the practice of receiving communion under both forms. They might need some instruction about this. It would also be wise to review the guidelines for receiving communion as presented in the missalette.

13. Make sure the couples check with the priest or deacon about special customs such as a presentation of flowers to the Blessed Mother.

14. Make sure the couples check with the priest or deacon before they print music booklets or other written materials. Explain to them about copyright laws and other things that might affect the parish.

15. Make sure that couples plan their music in consultation with the music minister of the parish. Please emphasize that the music at a wedding must be appropriate for a religious celebration, and that the music director can be very helpful in picking out good music. No one wants to deny couples their favorite music, but if it isn't appropriate for church, encourage them to save it for the reception.

16. Point out that some couples may prefer a wedding ceremony without a celebration of the Eucharist. This might be the best option for an interchurch or interfaith couple, or for a couple whose families do not participate in the life of the Church. The ceremony outside of the Eucharist includes the following elements: Procession, Liturgy of the Word, Exchange of Vows, Blessing of Rings, General Intercessions, Lord's Prayer, Nuptial Blessing, Special Customs, Final Blessing.

Note. Encourage the couples by reminding them that their wedding celebrations will be greatly enriched by prayerful planning and consultation. Careful planning of a wedding ceremony makes a strong statement about the priorities of the couple. Remember, the wedding liturgy is the public declaration of the faith of the new couple. Helping them to express that is a key element of marriage formation.

PART THREE

SESSIONS

SESSION 1

Welcome and Overview of the Theology of Marriage

As Catholics, we believe that marriage is a sacrament of vocation, a call to a holy way of life, and a symbol of Christ and the Church. Living the vocation of marriage requires that couples do their best to build a healthy, happy relationship, which takes time, skill, and information. This is one of the reasons why we emphasize marriage formation for engaged couples.

Despite the fact that *Unitas* provides an excellent start to a healthy marriage, most of us have met engaged couples who are uncomfortable about participating in it or in any Church program. The reasons for this are varied.

1. Some couples simply do not think they need any preparation—they know each other very well. What could they learn from the Church?

2. Some couples are Catholic but have been separated from the Church for a period of time. This is very common. Many couples today have not had an adult experience of the Church, and are therefore reluctant to return, especially if they think they have been forced.

3. Many couples are interchurch or interfaith. They are uncomfortable participating in a "Catholic" program because they are sure that someone will try to convert them.

4. Some couples have had poor experiences in the Catholic Church. They may generalize that the entire Church is like the place where they had the bad experience.

We must welcome all of these couples warmly. Whatever their reasons for being present at *Unitas*—and many are there only because they must be—parish leadership must make it clear that the entire Church rejoices because they take their future marriage so seriously. It is the responsibility of all working in *Unitas* to let these couples know that we are delighted to have them with us. For many young adults, marriage preparation and the desire to be married in the church is the natural first step (back?) into active participation in church life.

Furthermore, *Unitas* leaders must make interchurch and interfaith couples feel respected and welcomed, and demonstrate appreciation for the richness of the religions represented in the group. The non-Catholic partners must get a clear message that the Church is not trying to convert them. *Unitas* does, however, acquaint non-Catholics with Church traditions and beliefs about the sacredness of marriage. It also gives interchurch or interfaith couples an understanding about what the Church expects of Catholic partners in these marriages. Remember—we may be a non-Catholic's first acquaintance with the Church. We must make it a positive one.

Prayer for the Week: Jeremiah 31: 31-34

The days are surely coming, says the Lord, when I will make a new covenant with the house of Israel and the house of Judah. It will not be like the covenant that I made with their ancestors when I took them by the hand to bring them out of the land of Egypt—a covenant that they broke, though I was their husband, says the Lord. But this is the covenant that I will make with the house of Israel after those days, says the Lord: I will put my law within them, and I will write it on their hearts; and I will be their God, and they shall be my people. No longer shall they teach one another, or say to each other, "Know the Lord," for they shall all know me, from the least of them to the greatest, says the Lord; for I will forgive their iniquity, and remember their sin no more.

First Hour: Introducing *Unitas* and Introducing the Couples

The first hour focuses on introducing all the participants and welcoming the engaged couples to *Unitas*. It also serves as the time to introduce engaged couples to their sponsors, if you have not already done so. This hour should be friendly and informal. Couples will find the opening prayer in their workbooks and shall be encouraged to pray it throughout the week.

Session Objectives for the First Hour

- To provide a general introduction to *Unitas*.
- To introduce couples to each other.
- To begin building a community.

Outline: Welcome

Begin with a warm and friendly greeting from the pastor and the couples who will be leading the sessions. If possible, all involved in *Unitas* should be present at this session for introductions.

1. The pastor welcomes the couples and talks about why marriage is so meaningful for the Church community. He introduces other parish staff members and the *Unitas* leadership couples. The pastor should explain the roles of presenter and sponsor at this time. This should take no more than 5–7 minutes.

2. The engaged couples introduce themselves to the entire group. Ask them to simply state their names and their wedding dates. These introductions should take no more than 5–10 minutes, depending on the size of the group.

3. Engaged couples are introduced to their sponsors. See the ritual that pairs engaged couples with their sponsors on p. 44. This ritual should take no more than 10–15 minutes.

4. If the group is very large, the team breaks it into small groups: two or three engaged couples and their sponsors. Make sure the couples understand that they will be in the same small group for the entire process. The sponsor couples can take turns leading small group discussions when appropriate.

✍ Opening Activity: Priorities Exercise—What's in Your Wallet?

(Special thanks to the marriage formation team of Sts. Peter and Paul, Manorville, New York, for sharing this exercise.)

We have found this to be a fun, non-threatening way to learn more about the couples. You can do this exercise in the large group, or in the small groups that you have established.

Directions: Instruct everyone in the group to take three things from their wallets or purses:

- Something valuable
- Something worthless
- Something memorable

Each person explains why he or she chose each thing. The exercise serves two purposes:

- It tells something about a person's priorities.
- It gives couples a sense of the meaning of symbols.

This exercise can be very interesting. You will find out things that are meaningful or meaningless to various people. You will also discover differences in priorities among the couples. For example, one person in a couple might say that money means nothing, while the other person might say that money means everything. Listen carefully to what the couples say. You will be able to use their examples throughout the session's discussions. This exercise should take 20–30 minutes to complete, depending on the size of the group.

✍ Alternative Activity

If you find that you have some extra time at the end of the first hour, you might want to get some additional information about the engaged. Some suggestions for questions:

- How did you meet your partner?
- Where will you live after you are married?
- What do you like best about your partner?

Strategy for Session 1 when Using a BEGINNINGS Session

If you already have completed administrative tasks such as breaking a large group into small groups, matching engaged couples with their sponsors, and introducing the couples to each other at a formal BEGINNINGS session (see p. 42), begin Session 1 with the Opening Prayer, and the introductions of parish staff and married leadership. Skip to the "Priorities Exercise" (see above). Continue with the second hour discussion on the theology of marriage.

Second Hour: The Theology of Marriage

The second hour introduces couples to the theology of Christian marriage. This segment is central to *Unitas*, because it makes the case for the distinctiveness of sacramental marriage in the life of Catholics, and sets the tone for the spiritual dimension of *Unitas*. The engaged couples' experience and discussion form the basis for this conversation. Try to get them involved right from the start!

Session Objectives for the Second Hour

- To draw out from the couples the theology inherent in their hopes for marriage.
- To move from their hopes to the ideals of sacramental marriage.
- To introduce marriage as a sacramental covenant—distinguishing between covenant and contract.

Strategies for the Second Hour

1. Married couples who have tested *Unitas* note that many engaged couples are reluctant or resistant participants. Therefore, the introduction to the theology of marriage must be welcoming, non–threatening, and presented in language that the couples understand. *Above all, this is not a lecture that the priest or deacon gives.* If one of the parish staff gets up and lectures at the engaged couples about the sanctity of married life, you will lose them.

2. *Both* the priest and at least one couple should present this theological piece. The engaged couples must see that "theology" is not simply for clergy, but is a vital element in the lives of the married couples as well. Both clergy and married couples have something unique to contribute to the discussion on the theology of sacramental marriage. We suggest that commitment to their chosen vocation represents the common ground in the discussion. While it may be difficult for some couples and some clergy to present together, modeling collaboration in this session should reap rewards throughout.

3. One way to draw the couples into the discussion is to start with their experience. How do *they* understand realities like marriage, symbol, sacrament, and covenant? Drawing on the couples' experiences will help strengthen this session, and will set the tone for interaction that will be carried through the rest of the sessions

The second hour activities are designed to help couples see the connections between their ordinary experiences and the theology of marriage. The task of the discussion leaders is to get the couples to see that their hopes and their experiences are very similar to what the Church believes about marriage.

✍ Opening Activity: Couple Discussion

Ask the couples to find a corner of the room where they can talk with their sponsor couples (or by themselves if there are no sponsors present). They should take about 5 minutes to discuss the following question:

• **What do you hope for your marriage?**

After a few minutes of couple discussion, bring the entire group together for another 10 minutes of discussion. Write down the couples' responses on an easel or a chalkboard.

We have found that many couples hope for:

- Permanence
- Love and trust in their relationship
- Children (almost never now—but someday)

At the end of the discussion, remind the couples that many of the things they stated, especially the three qualities of permanence, partnership, and openness to life, are key elements of the Church's theology of marriage. The Church believes that marriage is a treasure for the couples and for the entire community.

> **Note:** If it is difficult to start this discussion, or if the couples don't mention some of the above qualities, the married couple should mention ONE THING you hoped for in your own marriage. (Any more than that and you might stop their conversation completely.)

✍ Group Activity: Discussion

Allow 10–15 minutes for this activity.

1. Ask the couples to help you define "symbol." Remind them that the things from their wallets were symbols—of their lives, of their experiences, of their hopes. Try to remember some of the symbols from the "Priorities" exercise; it will make this discussion very personal.

   Ultimately, you want to come to a definition such as this: A symbol is a concrete expression of something that we can't always touch. For example, giving red roses is a symbol of love. While we can't touch love, the red roses help us see the reality of love. Another example is a corner office in a corporation. Most Americans would be able to identify the big corner office as a symbol of power in an organization.

2. Encourage the couples to talk about symbols they know. Try to use these symbols throughout the discussion.

3. Ask the couples: **Is a symbol different from a sign?**

   The answer is yes—a sign gives a single message (a red, octagonal sign means stop). It is unambiguous. A symbol, on the other hand, has many layers of meaning. For example, red roses may be a symbol of love, reconciliation, or celebration. In other words, they may mean different things to different people.

Outline: Symbols/Covenant Presentation

This conversation should take 5–7 minutes.

1. Symbols make things present to people. They stir the imagination and the heart. They convey many layers of meaning without words.

2. Discuss the importance of symbols in our lives. One symbol in the life of a married person is a wedding ring—it conveys to us and to others the notion that we are in a permanent relationship; it may call to mind the memories of places, people, and events. For example, if I lost my wedding ring, I couldn't just replace it, because it carries much more meaning than the price of the gold. Help couples to understand that they are the most concrete symbols of marriage.

3. Help couples to see that when they join together in faith and love, they become symbols of a covenant. Help them to explore this idea. Begin with the following questions, and then lead into your talk on the theology of marriage and covenants.

✍ Group Activity: Discussion

Allow 10 minutes for this activity.

1. Ask the couples to define "covenant."

2. Ask them to explain the difference between "contract" and "covenant."

Outline: The Theology of Marriage

This conversation should take 10–15 minutes.

1. In a contract, we express rights and obligations. A contract defines the extent of one's responsibilities. If obligations are not met, we have legal remedies and recourse. In a covenant, we go beyond obligations to express unconditional love. A covenant calls people to be interrelated in love. It is founded in love and not limited by legal parameters

2. In theology, the covenant between God and God's people is central to Jewish faith. "I will be your God and you will be my people." As Christians, we believe that God's covenant with us was fulfilled in Jesus Christ. We, as the Church, carry out the work of Jesus Christ today.

3. Roman Catholic tradition states that marriage is a special kind of a covenant, which goes way beyond the contract. In Christian marriage, we are not involved in 50–50 relationships, but pledge to give of ourselves 100%. In a legal contract, if I do not complete my part of the bargain, I can be sued for "breach of contract." In a covenant relationship, each partner is willing to jump in for the other, knowing that the other might someday have to do the same. (An example would be good here.)

4. Catholics believe that we can make the step in faith to give ourselves completely to each other because God, through Jesus, is always with us. The idea of covenant is central for a theology of sacramental marriage.

5. After you have spent some time discussing the idea of covenant, explain that this is why we see marriage as a sacrament (a symbol of the Church). A sacrament is a symbol of God's covenant of love with us. In marriage, the couple is the primary sacrament. Through their lives, they embody the unconditional love of God. In a sacramental marriage, the faithful couple makes Christ present in the Church and the world. The "sacrament of marriage" doesn't automatically happen at the wedding day—couples grow and develop as the "sacrament of marriage" every day of their lives. In sacramental marriage, the couple is the tangible symbol—not only of their love for each other, but of their love for God, and their witness to the entire Christian community.

6. Sacramental marriage is not simply a private event in two people's live, it is an event for the entire Christian community. We all share in the joy when two people declare that they will be witnesses of Christ through their life together. Involve the couples by soliciting their feedback—and try to use it throughout the session.

7. Explain that all the sacraments are concrete expressions of God's love in our Church today. Some examples:

   • God's love for us is clearly expressed in the Eucharist. Jesus is present to us in the bread and wine, which has become his body and blood. We give thanks for the gift of Christ in the bread, the wine, God's word, and God's people.
   • God's love for us is expressed in initiation, when an individual is welcomed into the community of the Church and is called to lead a life like Christ's. (Perhaps some of the engaged are preparing for baptism or confirmation.)
   • God's love for us is expressed in Reconciliation, when we celebrate God's forgiving power in our lives.

You must remember that many of the engaged couples will not be familiar with this idea of sacrament. While some will be able to list the sacraments, they may not be able to explain them. Be patient! Couples will understand more about the sacramental life of the Church as they grow in participation with the community through *Unitas.*

The key in this hour of Session 1 is to introduce the ideas of our tradition in a way that the engaged can hear. If we lecture at them, or simply present them with doctrine, they will be unlikely to listen or understand. On the other hand, if we involve them in the explanations, use examples that will make the points clear, and present the content in an informal, non–threatening way, we set the stage for the weeks ahead.

Note: in Session 1, the time may not break down as neatly as you may like. Just be flexible; realize that you can't cover everything in one session!

Closing Prayer

Loving God, You have brought these couples here to grow in their faith and in their knowledge about marriage. Bless them as they begin *Unitas.* Help them to know that we, the community of _____, will be supporting them throughout their time with us. Strengthen them in faith, hope, and love, and help them to know that You are with them always. **Amen.**

Activity for the Week

✍ Couple Discussion: Symbols

The activity for Session 1 is designed to help the couples reflect on the meaning of the symbols in their relationship, and the importance of "covenant" in their marriage. Ask the couples to take some time this week to think about the following questions, and to answer them separately first, then to exchange papers and read their partners' answers quietly. They should dicuss their answers with each other, pointing out areas of agreement and trying to resolve any disagreements. Ask the couples to try to write a joint answer to the questions:

1. **What are some of the most important symbols in our relationship?**
2. **How have we experienced the meaning of "covenant" in our relationship?**

SESSION 2

Communication Skills

In this session, we begin to introduce communication skills that couples will need for their married lives, and continue to weave ideas about sacramental marriage throughout the session.

In any marriage, effective communication is essential. To be successful in marriage relationships, couples must be able to:

- Articulate their thoughts and feelings to each other.
- Listen effectively, to hear what the other is saying and what he or she is feeling.
- Understand that communication is both non-verbal and verbal.

In a Christian marriage, couples reveal the love of Christ through their love for each other. Healthy communication is one concrete way that they can develop a relationship that clearly reveals to others the love of Christ.

Communication in Christian marriage also involves forgiving and being forgiven. As part of the covenant of sacramental marriage, couples pledge to forgive as the gospel states: "seventy times seven" (Matt. 18:21-22). Communicating about pain or difficult issues is never pleasant, but it is part of our call—to grow beyond the pain to true reconciliation whenever possible.

As the development team reflected on this session, we decided to introduce prayer as a form of communication in Christian marriage. We believe that shared prayer is an essential element of marital communication. It not only opens our hearts to God, but it opens our hearts to the deepest place in our partners as well. Prayer is a unique form of relating to God and to each other that involves many of the skills that couples learn in developing other forms of communication.

Finally, in this session as in every other one, it is critical to remember, and to state, that the engaged are involved in a *process*. They will build effective communication *throughout their lives together*. While many couples already communicate well, this session will help them to strengthen their skills. On the other hand, some couples might experience real difficulties in communication. Let them know that you do not expect them to resolve all their communication issues by the end of *Unitas*. (If a couple has serious communication problems, however, you might want to refer them to the priest for further assistance.)

Prayer for the Week: 1 Corinthians 13:1-8a, 13

℘

If I speak in the tongues of mortals and of angels, but do not have love, I am a noisy gong or a clanging cymbal. And if I have prophetic powers, and understand all mysteries and all knowledge, and if I have all faith, so as to remove mountains, but do not have love, I am nothing. If I give away all my possessions, and if I hand over my body so that I may boast, but do not have love, I gain nothing.

Love is patient; love is kind; love is not envious or boastful or arrogant or rude. It does not insist on its own way; it is not irritable or resentful; it does not rejoice in wrongdoing but rejoices in the truth. It bears all things, believes all things, hopes all things, endures all things. Love never ends.

And now faith, hope and love abide, these three; and the greatest of these is love.

First Hour: What is Effective Communication?

This hour focuses on the principles of effective communication. It lays the groundwork for the second hour on negotiation. There is a great deal of content here; try to make it interesting by using stories from the lives of the married couples as illustrations of each point.

Review of Last Week's Activity

Review the take-home activity. Ask the following questions:

- **Did you learn anything that you would like to share?**
- **Do you have any questions about the activity?**

Session Objectives for the First Hour

- To discuss the importance of communication in a marriage.
- To explain that success or failure in any marriage relationship often depends on the quality of communication.
- To show that verbal and non-verbal communication are vital to the health of any relationship.
- To introduce the idea that forgiveness is a part of marital communication.
- To introduce the idea that prayer is an element of Christian marital communication.

✍ Opening Activity: Key Elements of Communication

Have the couples take a few minutes to complete the checklist in their Workbooks. After they complete the list, they can exchange answers and discuss whether they agree or disagree on these issues. Why or why not? Let them discuss their communication priorities with each other for 7–10 minutes.

✍ Alternative Opening Activity: Bad Examples

This activity should take no more than 10 minutes.

If any married presenters enjoy a little acting, you might want to try this activity as a way to stimulate discussion. The married couple begins the presentation on communication by stating the importance of effective communication in a marriage. Then, in the opening minutes of the presentation, the couple ignores as many of these skills as possible: cut each other off; use "you" instead of "I" statements; call your partner a name; bring up something from the past that is clearly irrelevant; don't listen to what your partner is saying; say something disrespectful to your partner; etc. After about two or three minutes, stop the conversation and have the engaged couples explain why this was such poor communication. Couples in the Washington, D.C., area believe that this is a very effective tool for starting the conversation on communication.

Outline: Principles of Effective Communication

This entire section, including all couple and group activities, should take no more than 45 minutes (approximately 20 minutes total for presentation pieces, and 25 minutes for the activities).

Team couples should remind the engaged that effective communication is a complicated skill that takes a lifetime to develop. We've heard people call it "the food that nourishes our relationships." In marriage, we are called to communicate on a deep level. This sort of communication, which expresses who we are—our needs, values, hopes, fears, and dreams—is complex and sometimes difficult.

1. We believe that effective marital communication is risky—because when we communicate our deepest thoughts, dreams, and fears to each other, we become vulnerable. Share an example that reinforces this idea.

✍ **Couple Activity** (3–5 minutes). Ask the couples to think about a time when they told their partner something they never told anyone else. Ask both parties to think about their reactions.

- What were the reactions of the partner doing the *telling*?
- What were the reactions of the partner who was *listening*?

Couples should share their reactions with their partners (and their sponsors if they are present). Do not ask them to share with the group.

2. As communication in our relationship grows, we develop trust and respect for each other. Share an example of how a sense of trust, respect, and equality grew as your relationship grew.

Note: The Church teaches that every person has the right to be treated respectfully in marriage. Marriage can never be an excuse for abusing one's spouse. Be clear—we can also abuse each other through destructive communication. For example, constant put-downs can be a sign of violence in the relationship. Abuse need not be physical or sexual to cause permanent damage. Effective communication requires that we not abuse each other with words, or the meanings behind words. Personal examples can help clarify these ideas.

---

3. Remind the couples that effective communication is a two-way street. In order to become successful communicators, we must learn to get a message across and to listen well. Try to share an example of how you accomplished this goal—or how you failed to accomplish it.

4. In order to listen well, we must hear both what our partner says and what he or she means. Listening to the meaning behind the words is critical in marital communication. Give an example of a time when you have heard a meaning behind the words or failed to hear it.

5. In marital communication, we must sometimes listen for double messages. Have you ever said to someone: "I feel fine," but your tone of voice or facial expression indicate that you were not fine? It is much more effective to say what you mean so your partner can get the message clearly. Give an example.

6. Good listening demands paying full attention to our partners. This means that we can't devote our energy to preparing a response—we must think about what they are saying at that moment.

✍ **Couple Activity: Discussion.** Couples should find a separate place for themselves and take 5-7 minutes to complete the following exercise.

• Think about something that is significant to you.
• Tell that thing to your partner.
• Ask your partner what you said and what you meant.

Wrap up the time by reminding couples that they can practice this skill any time.

7. In effective communication, couples must pay attention to non-verbal messages.

✍ **Couple Activity: Non-Verbal Communication.** *(This activity was first used in St. Mary's Parish, Colt's Neck, New Jersey. Thanks to them for their input.)* Couples should separate and write down all the non-verbal signals their partner uses when he or she is angry. (Take no more than 5 minutes.) After they make up their list, have them come together and describe their respective non-verbal signals to their partner. Let them compare their descriptions with their partner's list. Do they agree on their signals? (5 minutes.)

8. Over the years, we have come to see that forgiveness is an integral part of communication. We need to forgive and be forgiven when conflict arises, as it inevitably will. We think that relationships become stronger and healthier as couples work through their conflicts in a spirit of forgiveness and reconciliation. Give an example in your life where you have admitted that you were wrong and experienced forgiveness from your spouse.

9. In any marriage that is built on faith, shared prayer can grow and develop as communication develops. Developing a shared prayer life takes many years and much effort. Many couples do not pray together, or feel uncomfortable about praying together. Share an example about how you developed prayer with your spouse:

• Did it begin with mealtime prayer, shared worship, or shared Bible reading?
• How did it grow?
• How does it enrich your life?

Try to be very concrete in sharing the ways you pray together. It will help the engaged couples to understand its importance.

10. For interchurch or interfaith couples, shared prayer is a way to enhance communication about faith. Discuss the ways couples can share prayer, and can communicate about the similarities as well as the differences in their faith traditions. For example, Christians and Jews share reverence for the Old Testament. Catholic–Jewish couples can pray together with the psalms, the writings of the prophets, or the creation accounts in the book of Genesis, for example. There are many elements of faith that these couples share—help them to discover their common ground.

In presenting on each of these points, give concrete illustrations from your life. Presenting content by sharing your stories helps couples understand concepts very clearly.

Please remind couples that effective communication is a concrete way to witness the love of Christ in their lives. When couples communicate effectively, they teach by example the kindness, the care, and the love of Christ.

Second Hour: Negotiation and Conflict Resolution

The second hour provides a very concrete skill for the engaged couples—a methodology for negotiating. Couples will have the opportunity to practice this skill during this session and in the take-home activity. Point out that this skill can be used to resolve all kinds of conflicts in marriage.

Session Objectives for the Second Hour

- To demonstrate effective negotiation techniques.
- To practice negotiation skills that will enhance marriage.

✍ Activity: Role Playing

This activity should take no more than 10–15 minutes.

The situation is as follows:

> *Thomas and Mary are engaged and will be married next spring. This will be their first Christmas as an engaged couple. Thomas comes from a big, close family, which always gets together for Christmas. Mary comes from a smaller family*

whose members live in different parts of the country. This year, however, many of Mary's relatives are coming into town for Christmas day to celebrate the engagement. The families live four hours apart by car, so going to both places is impractical. How do they resolve the situation?

In resolving this dilemma, remember that the *how* is more important than the *what*. As long as both partners are satisfied with the outcome, there can be several solutions that will probably make everyone happy. Here are the ones we thought of:

1. Mary's relatives have come from great distances. Therefore, it makes sense to spend Christmas Eve (or New Year's) with Thomas's family, and go to Mary's on Christmas Day.

2. Invite Mary's relatives to Thomas's house for Christmas.

3. Spend Thanksgiving with Thomas's family and Christmas with Mary's family.

We're sure you can come up with other alternatives.

Outline: Negotiation Skills

This conversation should take about 15 minutes.

Remember—all marriage communication involves negotiation. Conflict in a marriage is not necessarily a problem—resolving it is part of marital adjustment. We can develop problems, however, when we don't communicate well enough to negotiate and resolve the conflicts. Even though we believe that Christian marriage is primarily a covenant—an unconditional commitment of love for each other, we also must realize that there are conditions—explicit and implicit expectations, rights and responsibilities—in every relationship. For example:

1. In marriage, we have certain responsibilities to fulfill for and with each other. One example: We will always be faithful to each other. Share an example of responsibilities from your marriage.

2. We also come to relationships with expectations and agendas—some realistic and some unrealistic. (Give an example such as this: "In my marriage, I expected that finances would never be an issue. . .") We enter into marriage assuming that our expectations will be met. Unmet expectations can cause difficulties in marriage relationships.

3. We all have needs and wants in our lives, and seek to have them satisfied by ourselves and others. When our wants and needs are not satisfied or resolved, we may experience dissatisfaction. Unfortunately, as we all know, no one can have all their needs and wants satisfied all the time!

4. As a result of our competing rights and responsibilities, expectations and agendas, we need to learn to *negotiate*—to resolve conflict so that both parties will be satisfied.

5. In successful negotiation we:

   • Identify our agendas.
   • Meet our own and each other's expectations.
   • Fulfill our responsibilities.
   • Satisfy our own and each other's needs and wants.

6. Negotiation involves a process of dialogue about an issue, an idea, or a concrete thing. Through negotiation, we usually get something that we want, but we also give up or let go of something in order to achieve the goal. In other words, successful negotiation creates a win-win situation through a process of give-and-take.

Creating Conditions for Successful Negotiation

In order for negotiation to be successful, couples must be willing and able to create the following conditions. They must be able to:

   • Identify what they want.
   • Treat each other with respect.
   • Be honest and straightforward.
   • Be willing to give and take.
   • Be open to the possibility that they might change as a result of the negotiation.

Six Steps for Effective Negotiation

We have found that effective negotiation is a six-step process. Using this process will help to clarify issues and find solutions to problems.

1. Clearly define the issues to be negotiated and write them down.

2. List points of agreement and disagreement.

3. Describe alternative courses of action.

4. Consider the possible positive and negative outcomes for each alternative.

5. Together, decide the most mutually acceptable alternative.

6. Together, make a plan to implement the decision.

✍ Activity: Role Playing

This activity should take about 15 minutes.

John and Jean have a problem. How can they negotiate this conflict? One of several ways it might be negotiated follows.

> *John and Jean have been married for two years. Jean is working in a dead end job to help the couple make ends meet. She couldn't get a job in her field, and is only doing this for the money. She is beginning to feel her biological clock ticking away and would like to have children before she's too old to enjoy them. John loves his career as a real estate salesperson. However, John's boss feels he doesn't make a good enough impression to sell upscale homes to customers. He is getting pressure to buy better clothes and a better car.*
>
> *One night, John is quite late coming home from work. He walks in the door with a suit bag in his hand and loan paperwork for a new car. He says to Jean: "I really need these things to get ahead." Jean blows up, and John can't understand why.*

1. Define the issues:

   • Jean would like a more fulfilling career and a baby. She thinks that John is being unfair in putting his career first.
   • John wants to be able to make more money so that Jean can take time off to look for a job, or maybe even quit her job after she has a baby. The better off financially they are, the easier it will be. His thinking is: you must spend money to make money. He doesn't understand why Jean can't see that.

2. List points of agreement and disagreement:

   • Jean and John agree that they want a baby.
   • They agree that Jean needs to get out of the job she's in.

- They disagree on the means. Jean thinks that by scrimping and cutting corners, they will be able to get what they want; John thinks that by making more money they will get what they want.

3. Describe alternative courses of action:

- John keeps the suit and buys the car. Jean will work at her job for a defined period of time to pay off some debts, and then they will try to have a baby and live on one salary.
- John keeps the suit and buys the car. In the meantime, Jean will start looking for a job in her field. When Jean is established in her career, they will try to have a baby.
- John returns the suit and doesn't buy the car. He and Jean will cut all possible corners so that Jean can afford to look for a new job and have a baby.

Obviously, there are other possible solutions. Brainstorm with the group to come up with the best alternatives.

4. Consider the possible positive and negative outcomes for each alternative. In each alternative above, there are positive and negative outcomes for work and family life.

5. Decide the most acceptable outcome. This will vary from situation to situation and from couple to couple.

Some Further Tips for Effective Negotiation

This conversation should take no more than 10 minutes.

1. When negotiating, focus on the issue and on each other. Try to deal with one issue at a time, instead of tackling a wide range of problems at once.

2. Don't try to interpret each other's feelings. Let your partner tell you what he or she is feeling. In marriage, we sometimes like to take on the role of our partner's therapist. It's not wise to do that. Leave therapy to the professionals.

3. Do not force family, friends, or children into taking sides in a marital conflict. This does not mean, however, that you shouldn't seek outside professional help, if necessary.

4. Use "I" instead of "you" statements. Notice the difference: "I feel terrible when I'm not appreciated," instead of "You take me for granted!" "You" statements tend to be accusatory.

5. Don't use words such as: "always," "never," and "must." They back your partner into a corner.

6. Don't give each other the cold shoulder. If you need space and time before you can resolve your difficulty, state that clearly—but ignoring your partner or refusing to resolve a conflict can lead to other problems.

7. If you feel an argument getting out of control, take time out. This may prevent you from saying or doing destructive things. While taking time out doesn't solve a problem, it gives you time to cool off and think about your position.

Make sure you use examples of these tips. Emphasize that at times we fail to communicate with love. Also note that some of these strategies might not work well in every situation. In general, however, they help facilitate better couple communication.

Closing Prayer

✍

God of Life, bless these couples who work to be open through communication. Be with them as they try to resolve their differences, and help them as they learn more about each other. Help them to know that You are with them during their time of sharing. **Amen.**

Activity for the Week

✍ Couple Negotiation

The activity for Session 2 encourages the couples to put the principles of negotiation into practice. Some time this week, they will sit down with their partner to discuss an important issue about which they can negotiate a solution. Suggest that they use the "Six Steps for Effective Negotiation" and the worksheets to resolve the situation. Remind them that successful negotiation creates a win-win situation because both parties are willing to give.

SESSION 3

⟨ornament⟩

Individual and Family of Origin

Before marriage, it is necessary for individuals to explore their personalities, values, and attitudes toward faith, heredity, environment and outlook on life. Each person needs to ask:

- **What strengths and weaknesses do I bring to a marriage?**
- **How might these strengths and weaknesses influence my marriage?**
- **How might they contribute to the success or failure of this relationship?**
- **Can you change someone else's personality?**

By exploring these issues, couples can grasp what they bring to their marriage relationship.

In addition to knowing themselves, couples need to be aware of the ways that their families of origin have shaped their development and can influence their marriages. While many couples believe that as long as they are in love, nothing or no one will affect them, behavioral scientists (and practical experience) lead us to a different conclusion: that families do affect us consciously or unconsciously. Therefore, awareness of individual family backgrounds is essential for building healthy marriages.

Knowing what we bring from our families to our marriages helps couples decide the shape that their relationships should take. This knowledge can help them:

- Choose traits, qualities and traditions from the two families that will be of value for their relationship.
- Work through family difficulties that can be passed on from generation to generation.

In order for marriage to be a concrete symbol of Christ, couples must be aware of who they are and what they bring to their relationships. Honestly exploring themselves and their backgrounds helps them to be open to Christ. We believe that Christ strengthens couples so that they can be fuller symbols of him through marriage.

In every relationship, two personalities join together to form a unique entity. The goal of sacramental marriage is not to lose one's individuality, but to bring it fully to marriage, and

· 81 ·

create something new. Catholics believe that Christ is at the center of this new creation. In order to embody Christ, couples must know who they are, and what they contribute to the union. Reflecting on these issues helps couples to appreciate the depth of what they bring to a marriage in Christ.

In this session as in every other one, we should remind the engaged that they are involved in a *process*. They will learn about themselves and the impact of their families of origin *throughout their lives together*. While many individuals are very self-aware, this session will help them to strengthen that awareness. On the other hand, some couples might experience real difficulties in figuring out who they are and how their families have influenced them. Let them know that you do not expect them to resolve all these issues by the end of *Unitas*. (Remember, though, if a couple is experiencing difficulty that you cannot handle, you should refer them to the priest for further assistance.)

Prayer for the Week: Psalm 139:1–10, 13–14, 23–24

℘

O Lord, you have searched me and known me.
You know when I sit down and when I rise up;
   you discern my thoughts from far away.
You search out my path and my lying down, / and are acquainted with all my ways.
Even before a word is on my tongue, O Lord, / you know it completely.
You hem me in, behind and before, / and lay your hand upon me.
Such knowledge is too wonderful for me; / it is so high that I cannot attain it.

Where can I go from your spirit? / Or where can I flee from your presence?
If I ascend to heaven, you are there; / if I make my bed in Sheol, you are there.
If I take the wings of the morning / and settle at the farthest limits of the sea,
even there your hand shall lead me, / and your right hand shall hold me fast.

For it was you who formed my inward parts;
   you knit me together in my mother's womb.
I praise you, for I am fearfully and wonderfully made.
   Wonderful are your works, / that I know very well.

Search me, O God, and know my heart; / test me and know my thoughts.
See if there is any wicked way in me, / and lead me in the way everlasting.

First Hour: Who Am I?

The first hour of this session focuses on the individual. Knowing oneself is a key component of marriage, because the more we know who we are, the more of ourselves we bring to the marriage. In this hour, shared stories are critical, because the content could become almost clinical in nature. Don't be afraid to share who you are with the engaged couples.

Review of Last Week's Activity

Review the take-home activity. Ask the following questions:

- **Did you learn anything that you would like to share?**
- **Do you have any questions about the activity?**

Session Objectives for the First Hour

- To discuss some basic elements of the psychology of human persons.
- To help couples understand that a strong marriage is based on self-knowledge and acceptance.
- To emphasize the belief that people are made in God's image, and to show how this belief affects our relationships.

✍ Opening Activity: Couple Discussion

Individuals should take about five minutes to think about and discuss the following situation for another ten minutes with their partner and sponsor couple:

- Remember the last time you faced a new situation—a new job, a new school, a party where you didn't know anyone, the first night of *Unitas*.
- How did you react? Describe your reactions.
- If your fiancé faced the same situation, how would he or she react?
- What do the similarities or differences about your reactions tell you about your personalities?

Note: The point of this exercise is that people react differently in the same situation, even if they are feeling the same way. These differences can be the result of temperament, upbringing, or education. You should be able to identify how you feel, and how theyu appear to feel.

Outline: The Human Person

Some ideas about human beings. It is best to communicate these ideas by sharing a personal example for each. This conversation should take about 20–25 minutes.

1. Remind the couples that we all have a variety of personality traits, which affect us in many ways. Every personality style has strengths and weaknesses. Couples must be aware of their own personality traits, and recognize their spouse's traits, to help make adjustment easier. For example, if I am a quiet, reflective person, I may consult you about a decision only after carefully thinking about all my options. That style may be totally different from that of an outgoing person, who always wants to talk about every aspect of a decision, and jumps to conclusions. Knowing the differences in personality style will help when you want to make a decision, but your approaches to it are like night and day.

2. Individuals are a blend of thoughts and feelings, heredity and environment. While heredity and environment affect people they need not rule them. All people have the power, within limits, to grow and change. For example, just because someone does not have every advantage as a child does not mean that they won't succeed as an adult, and vice versa.

3. Thinking is a set of processes that includes memory, problem solving, and creativity. It allows us to understand the world and deal with life's issues. We can solve problems because we have experiences that allow us to understand the issues and choose alternatives.

4. Beliefs are processes that imply things about us and what will happen to us. For example, if I believe that "I am ugly" this implies something negative about me and says something about what will happen to me in my relationships with others. Humans have many beliefs, and some say that our beliefs make us unique. To understand a person, one must understand his or her beliefs.

5. Within limits, humans have some freedom of choice. I can't choose anything that I want, and sometimes choices are not pleasant, but in every situation I do have choices. For example, no matter how hard I try, I will never be able to fly without a vehicle of some sort.

6. Because we have freedom, we have responsibility for our behavior and emotions. Thinking, freedom and responsibility are tied together. Choosing freely means that we recognize the connection between our choices and their consequences. A true choice only occurs if someone *understands* and accepts the connection that other things may happen because of their choices.

7. We have some power to plan and control our lives. However, many things are out of our control and we waste valuable time, effort, and resources trying to get control over them. For example, we can't control the weather, no matter what we do. Some people spend so much time and effort trying to change things over which they have no control that they miss many opportunities to do things they can control.

8. Above all, we can't change or control other people. People get themselves into trouble by trying to control the behavior of others. While we may be able to *influence* change or support a person when they want to change we have little hope of *controlling* them and getting them to do exactly what we want all of the time. For example, if you are trying to help your partner to stop smoking, forbidding them to do it in the house won't change their behavior. They will simply find other places to smoke!

9. People of faith believe that we are created in God's image. This means that we have a unique dignity. It also means that we have a unique responsibility to live as children of God.

Remember, people have power only if they take the time to understand what they can do, accept the responsibilities and consequences of their choices, and make the best choices that they can given the circumstances in which they find themselves.

✍ **Couple Activity: Who Am I? Who Are You?** Have the couple take about 5 minutes to list five strengths and five weaknesses of themselves and five strengths and five weaknesses of their partner. Let them discuss their lists with each other (and with the sponsor couple if they are present) for about 10 minutes. Discuss how they perceive themselves and each other.

An understanding of self, with one's strengths and weaknesses, is critical for a healthy relationship. Individuals should enter marriage with a strong, realistic understanding of who they are.

Second Hour: Family of Origin

The second hour focuses on the things we bring from families. Many couples do not appreciate the extent to which their families have shaped who they are. They also do not think about themselves as a new family, begun in marriage. It is good to look at our families, and figure out which of our family qualities we want to take into marriage, and which should be left behind.

Session Objectives for the Second Hour

- To communicate that we acquire traits and attitudes about life from our families.
- To communicate that we marry into families, with all their strengths and weaknesses.
- To communicate that we learn the first messages of faith from our families.
- To communicate the importance of personal, cultural, and religious traditions for marriage and family.

Opening Activity: Group Discussion

Divide the couples into groups, where they will choose two or three questions and discuss them for about 10–15 minutes. Give them examples to illustrate the questions. If individual couples wish, they can discuss unanswered questions with their sponsors at another time.

1. **What characteristics do we acquire from our families?**

2. **What did I learn about faith in God from my family?**

3. **What family traditions and customs will we pass on to our children? Which ones will we eliminate from our new family?**

4. **How much of what we learned from our families do we want to repeat in our marriages?**

Outline: Family of Origin

This conversation should take about 20 minutes.

Individuals learn many things from their families, some good, some bad.

1. What do people learn from their families?

> **Note:** You won't have time to cover all of these things, and some won't apply to you as a team couple. Just pick three to five points on which you can share your own experience, and perhaps make reference to some of the others. Couples will understand this best if you use some concrete examples throughout.

- What it means to be male and female.
- What it means to be married.
- What "permanent commitment in marriage" means.

- What role in-laws have in a marriage.
- What sexuality means.
- What faith means in a marriage.
- What money means in marriage.
- What role education has in the marriage.
- Which gender roles are part of marriage.
- How family and work are connected.
- How children are raised and disciplined.
- How grandparents and extended family fit into marriage.
- How physical, emotional, or sexual abuse has affected life.
- How alcohol, tobacco, or other chemical abuse has affected life.
- How a substance-abusing parent has affected life.

The point of this section is to demonstrate to the engaged that we bring our family experiences to marriage. If we are aware of what we have brought from our respective families, we can use that knowledge to strengthen our marriages. If we are unaware of the traits and attitudes that influence us, or if we are aware and choose to ignore them, they may destroy us. All of us, for better or worse, are influenced by the families from which we have come.

2. How do we address issues of family of origin? We must:

- Recognize the issues specific to individual families
- Discuss them and come to consensus about them

✍ Couple Activity: Family of Origin Discussion

Each couple should choose an issue from their families of origin that they think will affect their relationship. Let them discuss the issue and the way you will resolve it for 10 minutes. If the sponsor couple is present, they can discuss it with them.

Remind the couples that family of origin issues must be addressed early in a relationship. While couples will not always agree how to handle the things they bring from their families, they must be aware of them and communicate effectively about them. They must also be willing to negotiate about family of origin issues. Lack of negotiation about family of origin issues can lead to serious tension in marriages.

3. Becoming a new family. This conversation should take about 10–15 minutes.

- Sharing in a covenant marriage means that couples have the opportunity to become new families in Christ—beginning with their wedding celebration. Together, couples have the opportunity to build a family of love and faith.

Emphasize that couples become new families on the day of their wedding. Baby cards that read: "now you're a family" after the birth of a child are missing the point. A new family starts long before children arrive.

- Couples have the opportunity to build faith traditions in their new families. Together, they learn to *respect* each other's faith, to *challenge* each other in faith, and to *grow* together in faith. Interchurch, intercultural, and interfaith couples face the challenges associated with sharing two faiths. They must respect their differences, celebrate their common ground, and help each other grow. When children come—sharing different faiths will be a gift and a challenge for the entire family.
- The love created in the new family should move us outward. When couples are in love, they want to share it with others.
- At some point in many marriages, children will become a part of the family. In many ways, children embody the love of a couple. They carry the couple's love into the future, and put flesh on the idea that married couples are "fruitful."
- Be clear, though—having biological children is not the only way to carry love into the future. Discuss briefly the possibility of infertility, and the ways that infertile couples can share life with others. Give examples such as the possibility of adoption, providing community service to other children, or being a support for nieces and nephews.

Closing Prayer:

God of hope, bless these couples and their families. Help these couples discover the strengths and weakness that they have brought from their families, and lead them to peace in their hearts and homes. **Amen.**

Activities for the Week

✍ Self-Evaluation

This activity is not a personality test. It is a scale to help each person assess where he or she feels they are as an individual, right now. Participants will complete a scale by circling the number that best describes how they feel about each pair of words. After they have finished your sheet, they will share their answers with their partner. Ask the couples to share whether they learned anything new about each other.

✍ Family Traditions

This activity is designed to help the couples reflect on the importance of traditions and customs in their marriage. Couples should also consider the ways they agree or disagree about the meaning of family traditions and how they will (or will not) incorporate them into their marriage. They will be considering the following questions:

1. If I had to choose one or two traditions, customs, or attitudes from my family of origin what would they be? How would I incorporate them into our new family?

2. Do we agree on the things we would bring to our new family? Why or why not?

SESSION 4

Values in Marriage

What is a value? One definition is that a value is something that is held in high esteem. Another is that it is a principle that any group holds dear. A person's or group's value system is the set of principles that are at the center of their lives. Some core values for Christians are:

- Believing in Jesus Christ.
- Loving one another as God has loved us.
- Loving our neighbor as ourselves.

The integrity of our lives is intimately connected to the way we live out these values.

The first hour of Session 4 discusses the importance of values for couples preparing to marry in the Catholic Church. By choosing to marry in the Church, couples declare implicitly or explicitly that they are willing to accept and live by the values that are part of the Church's tradition. Our hope is that local Church communities will stand ready and willing to support couples as they put these values into practice.

Presenters should tie this session to the previous one on the individual and family of origin, because two of the key things we bring from our families are our values and a way to live them out. Whoever presents this session should be familiar with the discussion that took place in Session 3.

In the second hour of Session 4, we turn to a discussion of conscience. The Second Vatican Council stated that the voice of conscience calls us to love good and avoid evil. The voice of conscience is at the core of our being; it is fulfilled by the love of God and each other. Conscience leads us to search for truth—and for the solutions to problems that arise in our lives. (*Gaudium et Spes*, no. 16)

In contrast with this perspective, we have found that some couples today associate conscience simply with "do's and don'ts," or as a justification for doing whatever is convenient or easy. Our purpose in developing an hour-long segment on conscience is to help couples see that they are called to make mature decisions based on their values and in light of their informed consciences. We hope to introduce or reinforce the idea that an informed conscience, based on values, is a critical element in the life of the mature person of faith.

Developing values and a mature conscience is a lifetime project. Just as the couples grow and change together, their values and consciences will continue to grow and develop through time, maturity, prayer and work individually and together.

In this session as in every other one, remind the couples that they are involved in a *process*. They will continue to learn about their values and develop mature consciences throughout their lives together. Many individuals have highly developed value systems, this session will help couples to strengthen and share them with their partners. On the other hand, some couples might experience real difficulties in determining what they value and how they live according to those values. Let them know that you do not expect them to resolve all these issues by the end of *Unitas*. (Remember, though, if a couple is experiencing difficulty you cannot handle, you should refer them to the priest for further assistance.)

Prayer for the Week: Prayer of St. Francis

Lord, make me an instrument of your peace;
    Where there is hatred, let me sow love;
    where there is injury, pardon;
    where there is doubt, faith;
    where there is despair, hope;
    where there is darkness, light;
    where there is sadness, joy.

O Divine Master, grant that I may not seek so much to be consoled
      as to console,
    to be understood as to understand,
    to be loved as to love.

For it is in giving that we receive; it is in pardoning that we are pardoned;
    and it is in dying that we are born to eternal life. Amen.

First Hour: What Is A Value?

The first hour focuses on the meaning of "values" for individuals, for couples, and for the Church community. Couples will have the opportunity to reflect on their own values, and on their values as a couple. They also will be shown the ways that the Church can help support their values. Sharing your stories about the meaning of values in your life and the support you have received from the Church community will make these points very clear to the engaged.

Review of Last Week's Activity

Review the take-home activity. Ask the following questions:

- **Did you learn anything that you would like to share?**
- **Do you have any questions about the activity?**

Session Objectives for the First Hour

- To discuss the role of values for the individual and the relationship.
- To discuss the people and events that help shape values.
- To discuss the role of faith in forming values.
- To discuss the ways that a supportive Church community can help couples live out their values.

✍ Opening Activity: Group Discussion

Allow 10 minutes for this activity.

Discuss the following situation: You have just been offered a major promotion in your company. The problem is that the promotion requires that you move halfway across the country. What values enter into the decision-making process?

You might want to suggest some of the following values if you need to start the discussion. (Don't volunteer them to the couples immediately. Let them work this out!)

- Your career path.
- Spouse's career path.
- Being near family.
- Being near friends.

- The quality of life in the region where you live.
- Financial obligations.
- Support of a faith community.

Outline: Values

This conversation should take about 15 minutes.

1. Where do we get our values? Presenters can reflect on these areas and give examples of each to the engaged couples.

   - As children, we develop many of our values from our parents and other significant adults. Here, make the connection to Session 3.
   - When we reach school age, we begin to assimilate values from our friends and teachers as well. (What is "cool?" Who do we want to be as adults?)
   - If we come from a religious family, we develop values from the Bible, from our Church traditions, and from our faith communities. Again, connect to Session 3.
   - At some stage in our development, we accept some values, reject others, and begin to develop our own value systems.

2. How do values shape our choice of marriage partner?

   - Studies show that common values are a major predictor of marital success. We look for someone whose life vision is the same as ours. We also look for someone whose strengths complement ours. Give an example of how you and your partner's values and life vision are similar, even if your strengths and personalities are very different.
   - Serious marital problems can arise if a couple's basic life values differ greatly. For example, if one partner believes that the value of one's work depends on the amount of money one makes, that will greatly affect a job choice. If one person values faith deeply, but the other person doesn't respect religious values at all, the couple is likely to experience some problems as a result of the differences in their values. Make a connection back to Session 1. Ask the couples to think back:

     1. Did any of them disagree about the value of money or credit cards?
     2. Did any disagree about the importance of family of origin in their marriage?
     3. Did any disagree about the role of work in their lives?

     While differences such as these may not signal disaster, they do highlight the need for serious conversation and open communication.

- Every decision we make is a value decision. For example, if someone has the choice of a big wedding or a down payment for a house—a value choice must be made. Again refer to Session 1. Couples chose something from their wallets that was valuable and something that was worthless. How did those choices reflect their values?
- Willingness to make a permanent commitment is a key value for Catholic marriages. Do couples assume that this will be their one and only marriage, or do some think a marriage commitment can be easily made and easily broken?
- The value of giving life to each other in marriage is central for Catholics. How do couples give life by building up their relationship? How open are they to the possibility of new life?

3. How do couples' views of faith and Church affect the way they live out their marriages?

This conversation and the group discussion that follows should take no more than 25 minutes.

- What does it mean to share faith in marriage? Is faith a value in a couple's relationship? Are individual levels of faith similar or different?
- What happens if a couple's religious traditions differ? Is it possible to truly share faith in a two-church environment? It is particularly good if an interchurch or interfaith presenter can share on this issue.

4. How do Church communities help support values?

We think it is best to begin this topic through group discussion. Try the following format, and adjust it to meet the needs of your group.

✐ Group Activity: Discussion of "Church"

Each group should spend 7-10 minutes discussing the following questions:

1. **What do we mean when we say "Church"?**
2. **What role do you think the Church will play in your marriage?**

> **Note:** In this conversation, encourage couples to give honest responses. Some of them might be afraid that if they say something negative, they'll get in trouble. If the conversation isn't going anywhere, open the discussion yourself ("At one time, I thought the Church was .... Now I see it as. . .").

For people who are involved in their local Church communities, the answer to these questions are obvious—*we* are the Church. For many engaged couples, whose experience of the Church is sometimes very limited, it may mean various things. In class, we frequently hear students describing the Church as a building, Church as the place with the aisle where they will get married, Church as the clergy member who yelled at them once upon a time.

- Emphasize the idea that the Church is God's people, gathered in the name of Jesus Christ. Give an example of how you have experienced this reality.
- We know that at some times and in some places, people have viewed the Church simply as the hierarchy or the institution. The Second Vatican Council, however, emphasized that all who are baptized share in the life of the Church, and because of our baptism, all are called to serve the entire Church community. Give an example of how we serve God's people in marriage.

5. How can the local Church community help engaged couples support their values? Here, encourage the couples to discuss the ways that the parish has assisted them in *Unitas*.

Some examples:
- The community prays for the engaged.
- Sponsors from the community support couples on their journey toward marriage.
- There are activities and programs to help foster marriage relationships.
- There is a group for newly married couples.

These and other things might come up in the discussion. If your parish does not do these things, perhaps it is time to look into the ways that marriages and families can be supported throughout their life cycle.

✍ Couple Activity: Discussion on Values

Allow 10 minutes for this activity.

Each participant should take a few minutes to write down his or her top five values in life. They should then compare and discuss their lists with their partners and their sponsors. Remind the couples that they can continue the discussion after the session is over.

Presenters should conclude the hour by asking in general if people discovered anything new, or had anything new to think about. Get the general feedback from the group, but don't put pressure on the couples to talk about these things publicly.

Alternative Activity: Marriage Mission Statement

Developing a Marriage Mission Statement may be used in place of one other activity, if desired.

Many companies and other organizations such as parishes develop *mission statements*. These are usually two- to four- paragraph statements which try to sum up what the company or organization believes and how it tries to act. For this activity, each couple should take about fifteen minutes to develop an outline for a Marriage Mission Statement. Use these questions as a guide:

1. **What do you want your marriage to say to the world?**

2. **What couple actions best sum up your relationship?**

When they have finished, let them share their mission statement with their sponsor couple, and then take it home and work on it during the week.

Values help us to define who we are. What we hold as valuable will shape us not only as individuals, but in relationship as well. In a Christian marriage, the values of the Church community play a significant role for couples. Church communities have a responsibility to support couples as they try to live their values of faith and marriage.

Second Hour: How Do We Live Our Values? The Role of Conscience

The second hour is an extended treatment of the importance of conscience in our lives. The Church reminds us that conscience is at the heart of who we are, and helps us to make moral decisions in all aspects of life. In our experiences with young adults, however, we have found that many have not had a clear model for developing adult consciences. We think that this hour will give them the tool they need to build an informed, faithful conscience.

Session Objectives for the Second Hour

- To provide a framework for the concept of conscience.
- To explain the importance of conscience in the Christian tradition.
- To give practical suggestions for living out a Christian conscience.

✑ Opening Activity: Role Playing

This activity should take 10–15 minutes.

> *You have just been offered a $5000 gift certificate from a vendor used by your company. You have a large car loan, and your spouse has just been laid off. Your company also has a clear policy against taking gifts worth over $50. You come home and tell your spouse about this wonderful gift, thinking that he or she will be happy about your good fortune. Instead, your spouse is horrified, and says that you should immediately report the vendor to your superior because the reputation of your entire department is in jeopardy. What do you do?*

Note: As couples give solutions, ask them to consider the implications of each choice. What are some of the options for the couple? (Don't volunteer the following solutions, but these are some things that may come up.)

- Do nothing—but then ask: What will your spouse think?
- Confront the vendor.
- Tell your boss.

The point of this activity is to explore moral decision-making in the relationship. Are the values of the partners similar or dissimilar? How do their values compare with those of the Church community?

Make clear that Christians are called to a standard of decision-making that keeps Christ at the center. We are called to be like Christ: to be honest, to be life–giving, to have Integrity, to stand up for what is right, to strive to do God's will in all things. Moral decision-making takes into account all of these principles. (We state this clearly because some couples think that as long as they agree on an answer, it is fine. For, example, we have had couples state that it is acceptable to take the $5000 just because they agree that it is acceptable. Make sure they understand that it is not!)

Outline: Moral Decision-Making

This conversation should take about 20 minutes.

1. Moral decision-making is the natural conclusion of an informed conscience. What is conscience? While some think it is the voice that tells us "no," and some are

reminded of "Jiminy Cricket," the little friend of Pinocchio, according to the *Catechism of the Catholic Church*, no. 1778, persons are led by their consciences when they "recognize and act on the moral quality of concrete actions."

2. Does conscience mean that we just do what we think is right? No—much more than that is involved. It means that people weigh choices based on a number of factors such as the teaching of the Church, the advice of others, and reflection and prayer.

3. When is conscience important? Following our consciences is necessary whenever we are involved in a decision of consequence, particularly when there are costs and benefits in a number of choices.

4. How do Christians develop conscience?

   • Open yourselves to the will of God through prayer. Discerning God's will in your lives is a crucial step in forming conscience.
   • Gather as much information as possible about the situation involved. This includes finding out what the Bible says and what the Church teaches on an issue, and involves evaluating the beliefs and values that we have retained from our families, friends, education, and other sources.
   • Consult someone who can provide objectivity and insight.
   • If this is a decision that affects both parties in the relationship, make sure that the values of both parties are taken into account.
   • Be willing to re-evaluate the original decision if it doesn't seem to be right, or if conditions change.

5. How do we help each other develop conscience? As married couples, we have pledged to enter into a covenant relationship. We have promised to be "sacraments" or symbols of Christ's love to each other and the world. As we live in marriage, we grow in our ability to be symbols of Christ. We teach each other and support each other as we struggle with conscience issues in all areas of life.

6. Quote from the Letter to the Colossians (the Closing Prayer for Session 6 on p. 121): "Let the word of Christ dwell in you richly; teach and admonish one another in all wisdom; and with gratitude in your hearts sing psalms, hymns, and spiritual songs to God. And whatever you do, in word or deed, do everything in the name of the Lord Jesus, giving thanks to God the Father through him." (Col. 3:16–17)

7. What happens when couples, in good conscience, disagree with the Church's official teaching on an issue? According to Catholic tradition, an individual's conscience must take priority. However, this assumes that a person (or couple) has done everything in his or her power to form a correct conscience. He or she must follow the

steps—prayer, information gathering, consultation, and careful evaluation *before and during* the decision. If they have done all of these things, and still dissent, they must follow their consciences.

In Christian tradition, conscience formation plays a key role in adult moral development. In Christian marriage, couples are called to make decisions in the light of their mature consciences. Couples who have Christ at the center of their marriages must always ask the question: "What would Jesus do in this situation?" If we follow that principle in our decision making, we should be heading in the right direction.

✍ Closing Activity: A Celebration of Encouragement

This activity should take about 15–20 minutes, depending on the size of the group.

In this activity, each sponsor couple tells the entire group something they value in the engaged couple(s) they are sponsoring. They should try to say something about each person as well as each couple. Some questions to ask while you are thinking about the couple:

- What qualities does the couple bring to the relationship that you think will serve them well in their marriage?
- Why are they good for each other?
- Express some reason why you think their decision to marry this person is a good one.

After sponsors have made their comments, ask the engaged couples to share something they have learned about each other or something they have come to appreciate more about each other since the beginning of *Unitas*.

Closing Prayer

God of all love, please be with these couples as they work to discover and share their values. Help them to recognize You in the choices they make, and help them to know that You will be with them as they try to discern Your will. May You be at the center of all their decisions. **Amen.**

Activity for the Week

✍ Establishing Priorities

The purpose of this activity is to help each partner to clarify and articulate his or her priorities. Explain to the couples that in marriage it is important to know where your priorities are and where you stand in relationship to your spouse's priorities. After they have completed their individual ranking, they will try to achieve consensus in establishing their priorities as a couple.

SESSION 5

Intimacy and Sexuality

Growth in intimacy is at the heart of the Catholic understanding of married life. It is in becoming close, in sharing deeply, and in trusting and respecting each other, that we come to understand the reality of God. Experiences of intimacy in marriage occur in many ways throughout the stages of life. Developing intimacy, like developing other aspects of relationship, takes place over many years.

One way of expressing marital intimacy is through sex. Catholic tradition emphasizes that God has created man and woman as sexual beings, and our sexuality is a gift to be treasured and nurtured. Church teaching on sexuality highlights the intrinsic connections between life, love, commitment, and sex.

It is our experience that many couples, both engaged and married, have never really understood the Church's vision of sexuality and sex. Furthermore, no matter how much overt and implied sex we see all around us, most people are uncomfortable discussing either their need for intimacy or their sexuality. Even in a society where we see and hear about sex every day, we are not accustomed to addressing our attitudes and beliefs about these subjects.

For these reasons, this session can sometimes be difficult for both the engaged and married couples. It may become easier once its purpose is made clear. This session is not designed to provide "sex education"; rather, its purpose is to help couples understand their own attitudes toward intimacy and sexuality, as well as the Church's teaching on these topics. It is closely related to the sessions on communication, family of origin, and values, because so much of what we know about intimacy and sex comes from these sources. As adults, our attitudes toward intimacy and sexuality are linked to the values that we hold and those that we share.

It is crucial for presenters and sponsors to recognize their own attitudes toward intimacy and sex as they prepare this session. Some married couples are uncomfortable in this session—and it shows. For example, in an effort to break the tension, some married couples resort to jokes about "movies" or tell the engaged couples: "You can probably teach us a few things about sex." Those kinds of statements and jokes do not articulate the purpose of this session, which is to talk about our attitudes toward sexuality within the context of marriage—the intimate relationship most on the minds of these couples.

In our experience, we have found that even sexually active couples do not always discuss their attitudes toward intimacy and sexuality. The materials in this session should provide you with what you need to lead a discussion on these issues.

In this session as in every other one, remind the couples that they are involved in a *process*. They will continue to grow in awareness of their need for intimacy, their sexuality, and the Church's teaching on sexuality *throughout their lives together.* Let them know that you do not expect them to have full knowledge of all these things by the end of *Unitas.* (Remember, though, that if a couple is experiencing difficulty you cannot handle, you should refer them to the priest for further assistance.)

A Note About Session 5

In testing *Unitas* throughout the country, we have often heard that priests do not participate in this session because "they have nothing to contribute." We believe strongly that priests make a vital contribution to the discussion of intimacy and sexuality, and that their input should be encouraged by the married couples on the team.

It is not the role of the priest in this session to be the person who simply states the Church's official teaching on sexuality. Rather, priests should reflect on their need for intimacy, and how this occurs in celibate relationships. They also should discuss what it means to be sexual and celibate at the same time. Some of the most powerful sessions on sexuality in which we have participated have been those where the priest made a personal contribution to the discussion. The engaged couples, no doubt, have never heard a priest discussing his own sexuality before. The witness of a life that is both sexual and celibate gives couples a different perspective on fidelity to one's life commitment.

First Hour: Developing Intimacy

This hour centers around the need for intimacy in our lives. It will help couples become more aware of the various expressions of intimacy in their lives, and help them develop strategies to grow in intimacy. Through your sharing, you can help couples see that intimacy is not simply sex, but a 24-hour-a-day opportunity to grow in love with their partners.

Review of Last Week's Activity

Review the take-home activity. Ask the following questions:

- **Did you learn anything that you would like to share?**
- **Do you have any questions about the activity?**

Session Objectives for the First Hour

- To present a positive view of human intimacy.
- To discuss sexuality as an integral part of our personhood.
- To explore sexual intimacy as one element of an intimate relationship.

✎ Opening Activity: Group Discussion

Allow about 10 minutes for this activity.

It may take a bit of encouragement to get this discussion started. Begin by asking couples to consider the following questions. If it is slow in starting, you may want to begin with some of your own ideas about intimacy. Try to move the discussion so that these three questions are answered:

1. **What is intimacy?**
   Try to establish a definition: Intimacy is growing close/sharing time/trusting each other/knowing that you can count on the other. Many people use "intimacy" as a euphemism for "sex." Make sure that the discussion gets at the idea of intimacy as building a relationship.

2. **Why do you think it is central to a marriage?**
   If you need to, give an example here. "In our marriage, we have found intimacy to be central because. . ."

3. **How do you build intimacy in marriage?**
   We like to think about the way we built intimacy at the beginning of the marriage, and how that has changed over the years. You can share an example of how building intimacy is different after *x* years of marriage than it was when you were first married.

Outline: Presentation on Intimacy

This conversation should take about 20 minutes.

1. Intimacy is the basis of all deep relationships:

   • It implies trust and friendship.
   • It implies a knowledge of the other.
   • It involves a willingness to let yourself be known.
   • Intimacy in engagement and marriage should lead to growth in the relationship. An intimate relationship also should give individuals the support to reach out beyond themselves.

2. Achieving intimacy does not happen overnight. It takes time and effort.

3. Intimacy occurs in many different forms, such as:

- Emotional intimacy, which involves feeling close, sharing attitudes and dreams and fears, rather than just facts. (Remind couples about the discussion about communication in Session 2.)
- Intellectual intimacy, which involves shared work or hobbies.
- Spiritual intimacy, which involves shared faith, worship, and prayer.

4. A crucial aspect of intimacy in marriage is commitment. Knowing that another person is there to support you, no matter what, is liberating for an individual. That knowledge can help sustain a person through all the crises of life.

5. Recognizing the need for intimacy has always been part of the Judeo–Christian tradition. Genesis 2 tells us that it is not good for the man to be alone—therefore an equal partner is made for him.

✍ Couple Discussion: Beliefs and Ideas about Intimacy and Sexuality

This activity should be used no matter what else you choose to do. The self-reflection and discussion about the selected beliefs and ideas about sex and sexuality should take about 10–5 minutes—approximately 5 minutes to complete the checklist, 7-10 minutes to exchange answers. Do the couples agree or disagree on these issues? Why or why not?

Outline: Presentation on Sexuality

1. In marriage, a critical area of relationship is sexual intimacy. It is one of the ways that couples can share their closeness. Emphasize to the couples that everything we do is influenced by our sexuality—by the simple fact that we are male or female, and by the fact that we bring to this relationship various attitudes about sex. Sexuality is *who* we are—and sexual activity is a way to express our sexuality.

2. Highlight the fact that we all bring different attitudes about sexuality and sexual activity to our relationships. Remind the couples that they have learned many of their attitudes about sexuality from their families and friends, and these attitudes may vary considerably. (You can make a link back to Session 3.)

3. Even though we claim to be in a very open society—we see sex all around us—many people are uncomfortable talking about sexual attitudes and expectations. In marriage, it is crucial to communicate about sex, just as we communicate about all other aspects of life.

4. As a Church community, we believe that expressing sexual intimacy involves equality of the partners, not domination of one over the other. Furthermore, marriage is never an excuse to abuse your partner sexually. Any type of domestic violence goes against the notion of a marriage in Christ.

5. At this point, link the discussion back to Session 4 on conscience formation. Sexual decisions often involve awareness of values and conscience. Couples need to pray together, gather information, consult and evaluate their sexual decisions.

6. An intimate sexual relationship takes work:

   • Couples must take into account each other's needs.
   • Couples must work at developing a satisfying sexual relationship that grows through the life of the marriage.
   • Couples must be faithful to the marriage relationship.
   • At various points in the marriage, couples must plan for sexual intimacy. You will need to explain this. At this stage in their relationship, many couples won't understand why planning might be necessary. However, when children and their activities, work demands, travel, and a host of other obligations and responsibilities crop up, planning time for sexual intimacy becomes critical.

Alternative Activities

You will note that there are many alternative activities in this session. Presenters in some test parishes reported a need for some extra help in getting conversation started during this session. Pick and choose your activities. If something works, use it—and if it doesn't, leave it out. Your choices may vary from group to group. Don't be overwhelmed by the number of exercises—they are simply here to help you.

ℰ Group Discussion Questions

1. **What makes some relationships intimate?**

2. **Does intimacy mean that I "tell all" to another person?**

3. **In what cases might I withhold some information from a partner?** (If it could hurt the other person and is in the past, it might not be wise to tell them. However, if the partner could be involved, as in the case of a sexually transmitted disease, it is necessary to share that information regardless of how difficult it is.)

4. Does intimacy mean that I agree with almost anything that my partner says and does?

5. Does intimacy mean that I will always be "in love" with my partner?

6. Once I have achieved intimacy with my partner, have we "made it?"

7. Think about one married couple you know. How do they show you that they have an intimate relationship? Do they show intimacy the same way that you do? How do you think you will demonstrate intimacy in 15 or 20 years?

✍ Group Discussion Questions

1. What kinds of attitudes and values about sex did I learn from my family?

2. From my friends?

3. From society?

✍ Couple Discussion Questions

Have couples write down the answers to one or two of these questions. They should then share the answers with their partners. Allow no more than 10 minutes for this exercise.

1. How have we experienced intimacy?

2. Are there areas of our relationship where we have not begun to achieve intimacy?

3. Can we change those things?

✍ Couple Discussion Questions

1. How willing am I to discuss my sexual attitudes and values with my partner?

2. Am I afraid of sharing my attitudes and values about sex?

3. How will communicating about sex affect our relationship?

Role Playing

John and Mary are good friends of yours who have been married for fifteen years. They have three children and seem never to have any time for themselves. They're always running but not going anywhere. Their marriage seems to lack the spark that you feel in your engagement. What would you tell them to help them rediscover the intimacy they once knew?

Role Playing

You are the parents of a fifteen-year-old daughter (or son). He or she comes to you wanting to know what you think about premarital sex, and what you did about premarital sex. How would you discuss this issue with them?

Second Hour: Sexuality and Catholic Teaching

Many married couples report that this section of Session 5 is difficult to present because they think the engaged couples will be resistant to it, or because they disagree with parts of it themselves. Your purpose here is to clearly and gently communicate the Church's understanding of sexuality, which states that sexuality is a precious gift to be shared between two permanently committed partners. Some people will be surprised by what you say because they've never heard this teaching. Some will be moved to revise their own thinking and behavior about sexuality; others will remain unconvinced and will not change. Remember, you are not here to change people, but to *invite* them to see what our Church teaches on this and other issues.

Session Objectives for the Second Hour

- To present the idea that sexuality is a gift from God.
- To present the current Roman Catholic teaching on sexuality—which is far more positive than the pre-Vatican II teaching that so many of us were taught.

Opening Activity: Group Discussion

Allow 20 minutes for this activity.

Ask the group the following question:

- **What do you think the Church teaches about sexuality?**

Our experience is that many people do not understand the Church's teaching about sexuality. They think it is one word—NO!

Another bit of misinformation is that the Church teaches that sex is just for having babies. Once you get past the engaged couples' initial reactions, then you can start talking about the Church's actual teaching on sexuality. Because there is so much misinformation, it is critical to clearly state the Church's teaching on this issue.

Outline: Sex and Sexuality

This conversation should take no more than 25 minutes.

1. It is absolutely crucial to see our sexuality as a gift from God. God created us as sexual beings, who relate to each other as male and female. Our sexuality influences all we are and all we do. Give an example of how you understand your sexuality as a gift from God.

2. Many people are unaware or misinformed about current Roman Catholic teaching on sexuality.

3. It is true that throughout much of history, the Church saw sex as something to be tolerated, and not as a gift from God.

   • From very early in the Church's history, the celibate life was seen as a higher calling, and marriage was for those who could not be celibate.
   • Some believed that marriage was a distraction; celibacy allowed the Christian to devote himself or herself totally to God.
   • Some emphasized that sex was less than holy because it was associated with lust.
   • Up until the Second Vatican Council, the Church taught that the primary purpose of sexual intercourse was procreation.

4. As a result of the Second Vatican Council, the Church's official attitude toward sexuality and sexual intercourse changed. In the document entitled "The Pastoral Constitution on the Church in the Modern World" (or *Gaudium et Spes),* the Church affirmed that marriage is a holy way of life, and that sexual intercourse in marriage is a gift from God.

5. Since the Second Vatican Council, the Church's teaching on sexuality and sex has been positive and affirming.

Note: Please present the following teaching positively and gently. While we know from statistics that between 15–20% of couples support and try to live up to the Church's teaching on sex, many couples have already made their decisions about such issues as premarital sex and contraception. Despite this fact, gently challenge couples to consider what the Church presents in its views of sexuality—that sex is appropriate in marriage because of the total commitment made by the partners. When you personalize by sharing examples, you bring the message home to the couples.

- We are all sexual beings, created sexual by God.
- Therefore, sexuality is a gift from God.
- Sexual intercourse is one of the most complete gifts that one person can give to another. Therefore, it requires complete commitment. This is the logic behind the Church's teaching on premarital sexual intercourse—especially casual sex. If a couple does not share a permanent commitment, they should not give themselves totally to each other.
- There have been several non-religious studies that support the Church's teaching on sexuality. For example, some show that couples who live together for long periods of time are less likely to marry each other. This may be because they are having difficulty making a permanent commitment. For us, commitment and sexual gift-giving are inseparable..
- Every occasion of sexual intercourse has two equal purposes *which cannot be separated*:

  1. The love and support of the couple.
  2. The possibility of new life.

- This is why the Church teaches that every act of sexual intercourse must be open to the possibility of life. The contraception debate is not about "natural" vs. "unnatural." It is about the inseparability of the purposes of sexual intercourse.
- Therefore, the only legitimate form of birth regulation is Natural Family Planning (NFP). The reason for this is that couples using contraception prevent pregnancy in the presence of sexual intercourse. With NFP, couples prevent pregnancy by choosing not to engage in intercourse. While we recognize that many couples have already made decisions about contraception, it is still a necessary and good thing to present the Church's teaching clearly and completely.

Natural Family Planning

Natural Family Planning (NFP) is a method of birth regulation that relies on the careful monitoring of a woman's monthly menstrual cycle. By avoiding sexual intercourse during ovulation and the period around ovulation, it is possible to avoid pregnancy. Ovulation (when an egg is released from the ovaries) occurs 10 to 16 days *before* the beginning of a menstrual period, and is the time when a woman can conceive a child. On the other hand, planning intercourse during the time of ovulation can result in a greater likelihood of pregnancy, if that is the desired outcome.

NFP is not like rhythm, which relies on an average of past cycles to determine when couples need to abstain from sexual intercourse. Rhythm does not provide an accurate way to monitor monthly variations in cycle length, and is therefore ineffective.

Fertility Awareness as Taught in NFP

- When a woman gets close to ovulation, her basal body temperature rises slightly (by tenths of degrees). To determine when the temperature rise begins, it is necessary for a woman to take her temperature each day, before she gets out of bed, and record the temperature.
- As a woman gets close to ovulation, the secretions from her vagina change. They become wet and develop the consistency of egg whites to protect the sperm and help nourish it.
- As a woman approaches ovulation, the cervical os (the mouth of the womb) opens to accept sperm.
- Around the time of ovulation, some women experience individual indicators such as cramps, mood swings, breast tenderness, and changes in sexual desire.
- Reliability of NFP depends on careful charting and interpretation of these fertility signs, and a joint commitment to abstinence during the times of fertility (usually 5–7 days per month).
- The Church supports birth regulation using Natural Family Planning because it does not interfere with the inseparable connection between the two purposes of sexual intercourse—the love of the spouses and openness to the possibility of new life.

For further information on NFP, consult your Diocesan Office of Family Ministry.

Closing Prayer

God of life, help these couples to grow in intimacy and to be aware of the gifts of their sexuality. Be with them as they communicate themselves, body and soul, to each other and help them to grow in Your love. **Amen.**

A Note about Session 6 ("Balancing Practical Issues in Relationship")

A director of young adult ministry suggested that because the needs of groups vary so much, the engaged couples should be asked to decide which issues from Session 6 they would like to discuss. She thought the couples would appreciate the opportunity to shape the session.

Therefore, we recommend that **before the couples leave Session 5,** ask them to choose two topics for the first hour of Session 6 (see pp. 117–118 for topics). Try to reach consensus—but ultimately, let the majority rule. If a couple feels that their issue is not being addressed, suggest that they discuss it with their sponsor couple at another time.

Also let the couples know if you are planning a social event as a part of Session 6 (see p. 115 for details). For example, some parishes make this evening a covered-dish supper, with the engaged and the married couples contributing parts of the meal.

Activities for the Week

The Bull's Eye—A Model for Intimacy

Psychologists tell us that our life experiences are like a bull's eye. On the outside rim are the things that we share easily and with many people. As we move toward the center, we become more protective. Some things in our lives we share with very few people, and some things we share with no one. Marriage is one of the most intimate relationships we have. In marriage, two bull's eyes overlap to one degree or another. The couples will be exploring how much their bull's eyes overlap and how willing they are to be intimate with their partners in this exercise.

✍ Couple Discussion on The Catholic Church's Teaching on Sexuality

Couples will be writing about the following questions and exchanging their notes. Encourage them to try to reach a mutual understanding and lay a foundation for decisions about their married sexual life that is acceptable to both of them.

1. How do I understand the Church's teaching on sexuality?

2. How will this teaching on sexuality affect our married life?

SESSION 6

Balancing Practical Issues
in Relationship

In any relationship, the ordinary aspects of life sometimes receive little attention. However, realities such as household management, finance, and balancing career and family are of concern to newly married couples. In our fast-paced, high-pressure society, couples often are pulled apart by work concerns, school, and friends. Studies show that financial pressures are great, and frequently, it takes two salaries to attain a lifestyle that once could be supported by a single paycheck. To further complicate matters, gender roles are not clearly defined, which may lead to confusion in a marriage.

For couples beginning sacramental marriage, practical issues should be influenced by faith. In other words, how do day-to-day issues relate to faith values? Asking couples this question provides a context out of which to discuss these day-to-day issues.

While no single session will get at all the practical issues faced by newly married couples, we hope to make them aware of some of the concerns that they will undoubtedly face. Most couples have already encountered many of these issues, but they should deal with them in the context of their upcoming marriages. The discussion at this session focuses on the ways that both married and engaged couples have dealt with some of these very practical issues.

In this session, flexibility is the key. As *Unitas* leadership, you will know the couples and the issues that are important for them. Emphasize the elements that are most significant to your communities, but also gently introduce them to concepts that might be new or threatening.

In this session as in every other one, remind the couples that they are involved in a *process*. They will adjust to the practical realities of life on a daily basis. Let them know that you do not expect them to have all these issues resolved by the end of *Unitas*. (Remember, though, if a couple is experiencing difficulty that you cannot handle, you should refer them to the priest for further assistance.)

Prayer for the Week: Ephesians 3: 14–19

For this reason I bow my knees before the Father, from whom every family in heaven and on earth takes its name. I pray that, according to the riches of his glory, he may grant that you may be strengthened in your inner being with power through his Spirit, and that Christ may dwell in your hearts through faith, as you are rooted and grounded in love. I pray that you may have the power to comprehend, with all the saints, what is the breadth and length and height and depth, and to know the love of Christ that surpasses knowledge, so that you may be filled with all the fullness of God.

First Hour: Early Marriage Issues

This session is deliberately very informal. The activities are primarily group discussion questions and checklists for the couples to complete. At this point in *Unitas*, the groups usually are quite comfortable with each other, and have no trouble talking about a variety of issues. Especially in this area, the engaged couples can help each other by discussing their own strategies for resolving daily life issues. Some communities emphasize the informality of this session by combining it with a social event of some sort—a shared dinner or more substantial refreshments. You should decide this by the end of Session 5, and let couples know about the social plans ahead of time.

Review of Last Week's Activity

Review the take-home activity. Ask the following questions:

- **Did you learn anything that you would like to share?**
- **Do you have any questions about the activity?**

Session Objective for the First Hour

- To raise some practical issues that couples face early in marriage. In particular, household division of labor, finance, and shared traditions will be discussed.

Outline: Balancing Practical Issues

This conversation should take no more than 30 minutes, including the opening activity.

1. Practical household issues must be faced early in marriage. Issues such as chore division and the handling of money are usually divided according to personality and talent. However, expectations about gender roles and the division of household labor may have an effect as well. Couples should resolve practical issues through open communication and careful listening.

✍ Opening Activity: Beliefs and Ideas about Marriage Priorities Checklist

The couples should complete the checklists separately in their workbooks to help focus their priorities. It should take approximately 5 minutes to complete. When they are finished, have them exchange answers with their partners and discuss whether they agree on these issues. Why or why not? Allow 7–10 minutes for this discussion.

Beliefs and Ideas about Marriage Priorities

The married leaders should ask the couples to discuss their insights with the group, if they wish.

2. In working out differences about any of these practical areas, couples can use skills learned in *Unitas*:

   • Couples can use communication and negotiation skills to determine interests, likes, dislikes and expectations. (Remind couples of content from Session 2.)
   • Couples can use awareness of personality traits and expectations to determine suitability for tasks such as handling money, organizing records, etc. (Remind couples of content from Session 3.)
   • Couples can make value decisions to resolve major issues. (Remind couples of content from Session 4.)

Selected Topics for Group Discussion

(If you did not have the couples choose two topics at the end of Session 5, do so now.)

Allow up to 30 minutes for this activity.

Financial Priorities

1. Is "budget" a dirty word?

2. How do we define "necessity"?

3. What financial assets and liabilities do we bring to the marriage?

4. How much money do we wish to spend on leisure activity?

5. What role will saving money play in this marriage?

6. Is charitable giving a part of our value system?

Setting up a Household

1. Who does what chore?

2. Who does the chores we both hate to do?

3. Will we spend money to have chores done by someone else?

4. How do we negotiate behavior styles? (e.g., "He's neat and I'm a slob," or vice-versa.)

5. How do we spend our time together? (Watching football, playing golf, shopping, etc.)

6. Will long commutes be a part of our life together?

7. Is buying a house a priority?

8. Is a house a necessity before a baby?

Other Relationships in the First Year of Marriage

1. How much time should we spend with our extended families?

2. How do we plan for holidays?

3. How much time will we spend with our friends?

4. Do all social activities take place with my spouse?

5. Do I make social plans with friends independent of my spouse?

✍ Sharing Faith

1. Is faith an important value in my life?

2. Do we share faith?

3. Do we agree on how we express faith?

4. How will we deal with it if we disagree on the importance of faith?

5. If our faith traditions differ, how do we celebrate them in our family?

6. If our faith traditions differ, what will our wedding ceremony look like?

7. If our faith traditions differ, how we will raise our children?

Second Hour: Work and Family—A Balancing Act

When we were developing *Unitas*, many people from across the country suggested that we include an entire section on the two-income household. We took this advice seriously, and tried to provide food for thought about this ever-growing phenomenon. One thing we have noticed, however: Sometimes, the presenters or sponsor couples believe that it is better for the husband to be the breadwinner and the wife to be the homemaker, especially after children arrive. Please note that many engaged couples do not agree with this position. This section is not about convincing them to change their minds; it is about helping them come to terms with balancing work and family in today's society.

Session Objectives for the Second Hour

- To discuss the role of work in today's family.
- To address the issue of the dual career family in today's society.
- To discuss the relationship of gender roles, family and work in today's society.

✍ Couple Activity: Beliefs and Ideas about Work and Career Checklist

Have the couples complete their respective checklists to help them focus their thinking about work and career.

Each person should take approximately 15 minutes to complete the checklist. When they are finished, have them exchange answers with their partners and discuss whether they agree or disagree on these issues. Why or why not? Have them discuss their priorities with each other for 7–10 minutes. Afterwards, you may ask the couples to discuss their insights with the group, if they wish.

Outline: Balancing Careers and Family

Allow up to 20 minutes for this conversation.

> **Note:** There are no right or wrong answers here. What is life-giving to the marriage must take priority.

1. There are several different ways that couples can look at the relationship between marriage and work.

   • In some families, one partner will be the sole wage earner and the other will work primarily at building the home. This arrangement assumes that one partner can support the family, and that the other partner is willing and able to work primarily in the home. Of course, today many people can continue jobs or careers from a home office, allowing considerable flexibility for partners.
   • "Dual jobs" means that both partners will work outside the home to one extent or another. This does not mean, however, that both partners have equal commitments to their jobs. One person might be in a career, while the other may simply be trying to earn a little extra money to make ends meet. In this situation, one person's job may take priority over the other.
   • One partner may be willing and able to take a job with flexible hours, even if the pay is very low.
   • "Dual career" means that both partners' work involves a considerable investment of time and effort, and that their jobs will be more than simply a means to make money.
   • "Dual career" couples must ask difficult questions about the relationship between family life and work life.
   • Some couples choose to make career sacrifices when children are born. One partner may defer a career for a number of years in order to make childrearing a priority.

2. Help the couples to see that gender expectations often color decisions about careers and jobs. Ask the following questions about the relationships between gender, work, and family. For example:

- Whose career has priority?
- Are earning power and decision making linked?
- Does gender affect the answers to the above questions?

These are just a few questions that couples must address as they navigate the complex waters of work and family.

In this area, as in so many others, there is no one right answer to these questions. Couples must explore their goals and values, their expectations and their life objectives, in order to answer these questions. Career is a crucial issue for many couples, and it is a good thing to explore it in a non-threatening, informal context.

✍ Group Activity: Discussion

Allow about 20 minutes for this activity.

Some of these questions may be used to start a discussion about balancing work and career.

- How easy is it to maintain a "two-career household?"
- What do you think it would take to do so?
- Are men's and women's careers really equal?
- Is the value of a career dependent on how much money the person makes?
- How easy is it to care for children in a two-career household?
- Which comes first, work or family? How do you decide?

If you have other questions, please feel free to substitute or add them.

Activity for the Week

✍ FOCCUS Follow-up: Balancing Practical Issues

The purpose of this activity is to help focus the couples' attention on issues that may arise early in marriage. While some of the questions may seem simple, answering them can present some surprising (and sometimes disturbing) results. Remind the couples to recall their

FOCCUS inventories, and to address first those questions that pertain to the issues raised by FOCCUS that are unresolved. Encourage them to find consensus.

Discussion Questions:

1. What are our financial priorities?

2. How will we set up our household?

3. How will we balance other relationships in the first year of marriage?

4. How will we integrate faith into our daily lives?

5. How will we balance career and family?

Closing Prayer: Colossians 3:12–17

As God's chosen ones, holy and beloved, clothe yourselves with compassion, kindness, humility, meekness, and patience. Bear with one another, and if anyone has a complaint against another, forgive each other; just as the Lord has forgiven you, so you must also forgive. Above all, clothe yourselves with love, which binds everything together in perfect harmony. And let the peace of Christ rule in your hearts, to which indeed you were called in the one body. And be thankful. Let the word of Christ dwell in you richly; teach and admonish one another in all wisdom; and with gratitude in your hearts sing psalms, hymns, and spiritual songs to God. And whatever you do, in word or deed, do everything in the name of the Lord Jesus, giving thanks to God the Father through him. **Amen.**

SESSION 7

Developing a
Spirituality of Marriage

We strongly believe that the spirituality of marriage and the family is grounded in ordinary life. Therefore, it is intimately connected with our ability to communicate, to recognize where we have come from, to share values, and to relate intimately with each other. As Christians, we are called to grow in awareness of ourselves as holy people, created in God's image and likeness. This session focuses on the sacredness of ordinary life and the need to create centers of faith in our hearts and in our homes.

In this session, keep in mind that many of these couples do not identify themselves as spiritual people. Help them recognize the spiritual dimensions that are already present in their lives. It is also critical to help them see that growth in spirituality, as growth in all other areas of life, is a process that takes a lifetime to accomplish. Encourage the engaged to look at where they are now and give them strategies to help them grow in spirituality.

In this session as in every other one, remind the couples that they are involved in a *process*. They will continue to grow in their spirituality *throughout their lives together*. Even though some individuals have a highly developed spirituality, this session will help couples to strengthen it and share it with their partners. On the other hand, some couples might experience real difficulties in articulating their spirituality. Let them know that you do not expect them to resolve all these issues by the end of *Unitas*. (Remember, though, if a couple is experiencing difficulty that you cannot handle, you should refer them to the priest for further assistance.)

First Hour: Defining "A Spirituality of Marriage"

The first hour of this session centers on the idea that spirituality is an integral part of daily life. Many couples will be surprised to hear that we understand spirituality in a way that goes beyond church attendance and formal prayer. Show them by your examples that you believe spirituality is as much a part of who we are as breathing is. Help them to see that we can become closer to God through daily activities.

Review of Last Week's Activity

Review the take-home activity. Ask the following questions:

- **Did you learn anything that you would like to share?**
- **Do you have any questions about the activity?**

Session Objectives for the First Hour

- To encourage couples to think about what "spirituality of marriage" means in their lives.
- To help connect spirituality with all content areas of *Unitas*. In each session, couples have discussed the ways that each element of marriage is connected to faith. Session 7 reminds couples of all the ways they have been developing their spirituality throughout the process.
- To facilitate discussion about how spirituality can be lived in married life. Focus will be on shared prayer, shared worship, and shared faith values.

✍ Opening Activity: Group Discussion

Discuss this question in small or large groups for about 5–10 minutes.

- **What makes a spiritual person?**

> **Note:** We have found that typical answers to this question usually center around religion. Couples define "spirituality" as going to church, reading the Bible, saying your prayers, etc. Very few couples get at the idea that spirituality also is reflected in the very ordinary things of life. After they have discussed this question, let them complete the checklist, which will give them a very different perspective on spirituality.

✍ Couple Activity: What Helps Me to Develop My Spirituality?

The point of this exercise is to show that married people develop their spiritual lives in many ordinary activities of life. Marriage demands that we love unconditionally, that we trust God in good times and bad times, that we make sacrifices for others as Jesus did, and that we die to ourselves for the greater good of the relationship and family. Any one of the above activities can provide opportunities for spiritual growth, and different things will be important to different people.

✍ Alternative Activity: Couple Discussion

Allow 10–15 minutes for this activity.

Have the engaged couples move to separate places with their sponsors if they are present at the session.

1. The couples should write down three to five characteristics of their spirituality as they experience it now.

2. Next, they should write down three to five ways that they can grow in spirituality over the next two years.

3. Let the couples share their answers with their sponsors, who can share suggestions and strategies for building spirituality in their marriages.

Outline: The Spirituality of Marriage

This conversation should take about 15 minutes.

Don't forget to discuss these areas by using personal examples. This will help couples to see concretely what you mean by "spirituality of marriage."

1. In the first hour, the focus is on demonstrating that "spirituality" is a way of life that keeps God at the center of all we do.

2. Marriage gives us many opportunities to be spiritual people through concrete actions. Our spirituality is not simply defined by the number of hours we spend in church, but by the way we treat our spouses, children, extended families and friends as "other Christ's." We also share our spirituality by praying at home together and worshipping together.

3. Emphasize once again that Catholics believe marriage is a covenant and a sacrament. (Remind the couples of the discussion in Session 1.) This means that, as a couple, we choose to embody Christ in our day-to-day lives. While no one can be like Christ perfectly, sacramental couples are called to be like Christ in the way they treat their families and friends, in the way they conduct themselves in the workplace, and in the way they relate to each other. Christ is always central in a sacramental marriage.

4. Remind couples that sacramental marriage is a vocation in the Church (from the Latin, *vocare*, to call) just as religious life is a vocation. When couples say yes to Christian marriage, they make a daily commitment to love each other as Christ loves us. Christian marriage is not something that simply happens on the wedding day, it is something that we live every day. When couples stop working on their vocation, difficulties frequently arise.

5. Help couples to see that through baptism, we are called to be witnesses of Christ and the Church in the world. Couples may need to be reminded that they serve as witnesses of Christ through their marriage. Their holiness does not occur *in spite of* their marriage, it happens *in* and *through* their marriage.

6. Help couples to see that by living their vocation, Christian married couples have the opportunity to "build faith" in their homes. Introduce the idea that the family is a center of faith. This means that we are always aware that the ordinary things of family life can be holy when motivated by the love of Christ.

7. Help couples to see that the ways they express their faith together will have an impact for their marriage. Remind them that differences in faith do not only occur among interchurch or interfaith couples. Many Catholic couples must address the issues that arise when one party practices his or her faith and the other does not. This situation is very common among Catholic couples.

8. Help interchurch, intercultural, and interfaith couples to recognize that they have the opportunity to build centers of faith in their homes by working to share their religious traditions. Interchurch and interfaith marriages present unique challenges and can be greatly enriched by sharing the variety of traditions present in a family.

✍ Couple Activity: Spirituality Discussion

Allow 15 minutes for this activity.

Have the couples separate for about 5 minutes to think about the last few weeks of their lives. List five things that they have done as a couples to build their spirituality. For example:

- Have you as a couple reached out to another person?
- Have you participated openly in *Unitas?*
- Have you spent significant time with each other?

Let them share these things with each other and with their sponsor couple.

✍ Alternative Group Discussion Questions

1. Who is the most spiritual person you know?

2. How has that person affected your life?

3. How will you live spirituality in marriage?

4. Has your view of marriage as covenant and sacrament changed over the course of your marriage formation?

Second Hour: Building Faith in Families

Many people have not thought about the ways they can build faith in their families on a daily basis. Help the couples to see that the smallest unit of faith is the family, not the parish. In other words, we bring our small faith community to the larger Church. Let the couples know that this idea has a long tradition in our Church's history. When you build up your families, you have the possibility of building up the Church as well.

Session Objectives for the Second Hour

- To introduce the idea that we build our families as centers of faith.
- To give concrete examples of living faith in day to day family life.

✍ Opening Activity: Building Church in Our Homes

(This activity reflects the insights of the marriage formation team at St. Aidan's Parish, Williston Park, N.Y. Thanks to them for sharing it.)

Allow 15–20 minutes for this activity.

For this activity, you will need one pack of 3 x 5 index cards and pens. The activity is designed to help couples set priorities for the five most important elements of a faith-filled family.

Divide the large group into small groups of no more than four couples. If sponsor couples are present, this means two engaged couples and two married couples. Ask the following question: **What elements belong in a church of the home?**

1. Each person should take five index cards and write on each card one thing that is essential for a faith-filled family.

2. After everyone has completed five cards, share the cards with the group.

3. The group should classify the cards and eliminate duplicates.

4. Lay out the cards so that you build your "church of the home."

5. Be sure to arrange the cards in the order and the shape that you want them!

After the groups are finished, ask the question: How do you think these elements of faith-filled families help to build the larger Church community? Do you think they are priorities for the larger Church as well? Discuss it with the entire group for 5–10 minutes.

✍ Follow-Up Activity: Group Discussion

Allow 15-20 minutes for this activity.
Explore one or more of the following questions:

1. How do you share prayer when there are differences in tradition?
2. How do you share holidays when there are differences in tradition?
3. How do you respect each other's faith?
4. How do you raise children in two different traditions?
5. Is one of you thinking about conversion?

> **Note:** If there are several interchurch or interfaith couples in the group, it is necessary to explore their vision of a "faith-filled family." How do they build faith-filled families in the context of different traditions? Some or all of these discussion questions can be used if you have a large percentage of interchurch or interfaith couples in the group. They also can be used as individual questions for sponsor couples if they are working with interchurch or interfaith couples. Allow about 10 minutes for this activity.

Outline: Building Faith in Our Families

This conversation should take about 20 minutes.

1. Remind the couples about an idea from Session 3, that family begins with the new marriage, and not with children. Couples begin to build traditions, shared values, and faith as soon as they begin to share a household after marriage. Discussing this idea helps couples understand that faith can be shared in the home at any time.

2. Building faith in our families implies that we take special care to find God in all we do, and that we work to build faith through the ordinary things of our lives. In the simple, day-to-day experiences of life, we have the opportunity to be like Christ for our spouses and for others.

3. Explain to couples how you have experienced faith in your family of origin and in your family now. Share some concrete celebration of faith from your home. Welcoming rituals for new family members, birthday and anniversary celebrations and other family times can be opportunities for faith sharing.

4. Discuss the idea that building faith in families is a strong part of recent Catholic tradition. For example, Pope John Paul's document *Familiaris Consortio*, the U.S. Bishops' *A Family Perspective in Church and Society*, and the Pontifical Commis-

sion on the Family's *Guidelines for Marriage Preparation* state that Christian families are called to build faith in their homes and reach out to the larger Church and world. (**Note:** You don't have to give them all these titles—they'll think they're in a classroom.)

5. *Familiaris Consortio* and *A Family Perspective in Church and Society* state that the Christian family is called to accomplish four tasks that build faith in families. While others could be included, we believe that these tasks communicate the essence of what it means to live faith in our homes. Use examples of how you try to live out each one of these tasks in your own homes.

   • **Faith-filled families form a community of persons.** This means that couples are called to build a partnership of love and life in marriage. Remind the couples that forming a community of persons includes concepts that they have worked on in *Unitas* including:

      1. Trust and respect for each other.
      2. Effective communication.
      3. Building intimacy in marriage.

   • **Faith-filled families serve life in many ways,** such as:

      1. Having children and educating them. For some couples, this may mean welcoming a child into their homes through adoption or foster care or being a "parent" to children in the community.
      2. Communicating respect for life to others. This may mean taking a stand on issues such as assisted suicide, abortion, unemployment, immigration, housing or a host of others.
      3. Making sacrifices so that life is protected.
      4. Living in a way that supports the principle that says all life is sacred whether a person is rich or poor, young or old, educated or uneducated.

   • **Faith-filled families build up society by reaching beyond our own little communities to make the world a better place.** We can achieve this goal by:

      1. Demonstrating collaboration and shared decision-making in the family. Give an example of how you do this in your families. Things such as family meetings and age-appropriate responsibility are some ways that this can happen.
      2. Fostering civic responsibility through involvement in the community. Give an example such as voting, campaigning for a candidate, paying taxes, etc.
      3. Promoting care for the earth. Give an example such as participating in Earth Day celebrations or recycling.

- **Faith-filled families share in the mission and life of the Church.** Families must recognize and understand that *they* are the Church. However, no one is Church in isolation. We are part of a larger community locally, and part of a universal Church. We share in the mission of the Church on many levels. In our homes, we are called to recognize that in very ordinary events of our lives, we make Christ present. For example:

    1. When we let go of something and "die" to ourselves so that someone else might have a better life, we enter into Christ's death and resurrection.
    2. When we welcome a child or adult into our families, we share in the Rites of Initiation that our Church celebrates.
    3. When we share a family meal, give thanks, and take time to recall who we are, we parallel the Eucharist in our homes.
    4. When we forgive and are forgiven, the ministry of Reconciliation becomes a part of our family life.

These are just some examples—there are many more. Each day of our lives, we share in the mission of the Church by participating in the community and by being Church in our day-to-day lives.

Building faith in our homes is a way of life. It takes commitment, time and effort. It is something that grows over the life of the family. It doesn't happen magically on a wedding day, but takes a life of working together for the good of each other, the family, the local community and the Church community. It is not something that many engaged couples think about, but it is a goal that they can attain with their love, and the support of their family, friends, and faith community.

✍ Alternative Group Discussion Questions

1. How do you think you will create a faith-filled family?

2. What family traditions can you create that will foster faith in your family?

3. What are some ways that you as a couple can bring the message of Christ to others?

4. How can you share time and talent as married couples in the Church community?

5. If you are two different religions, how will you build faith in your home?

Conclusion

Thank couples for their participation in the sessions and invite them to the special activities that will take place in the parish.

Remind them that there will be a special celebration at a Sunday liturgy, and a reception to follow. Make sure they know that they can invite their families as well.

Remind them to complete their evaluations (located at the end of the Couple's Workbook) and bring them to the final celebration.

Finally we have developed this prayer service to conclude Session 7. Please feel free to substitute another service if you choose.

Session Closing Prayer

Leader: In the name of the Father, and of the Son, and of the Holy Spirit. **All:** Amen.

Leader: Let us Pray. **Life-giving God,** we thank You for your gifts, especially the gift of these engaged and married couples. Help them to grow in faith and love for each other and You. Be with them today and throughout their married lives. We make this prayer through Christ our Lord, Amen.

Scripture Reading: John 15:9–12

"As the Father has loved me, so I have loved you; abide in my love. If you keep my commandments, you will abide in my love, just as I have kept my Father's commandments and abide in his love. I have said these things to you so that my joy may be in you and that your joy may be complete. This is my commandment, that you love one another as I have loved you."

Leader: The Gospel of the Lord. **Response:** Praise to you, Lord Jesus Christ

Intercessions: The response to our prayers is: God of life, hear our prayer.

- For the Church, which stands as a light of hope in the midst of the world, we pray:
- For the world, which needs strong witnesses of love, we pray:

- For the poor and powerless in our midst, that God will provide for them, we pray:
- For all married couples, especially those who are struggling, we pray:
- For our families and friends, that we may live in peace with them, we pray:
- For all couples preparing for marriage, that they may grow in love and commitment, we pray:
- For any prayers that you would like to share: (pause) we pray:

Reflection: Ask participants to take a few minutes to share their reflections on *Unitas*.

Leader: Let us conclude our prayer today by joining hands and praying in the words that Jesus gave us. Our Father...

Final Blessing: May God bless us and keep us.
May God's face shine upon us.
May God look upon us kindly and give us peace.

Amen.

Activity for the Week

℘ Giftedness

This activity is designed to help the participants claim their gifts and to see the relationship between what they do at home and what they can do in the community of the Church.

PART FOUR

TEAM
EVALUATION
OF UNITAS

Team Evaluation of Unitas

✍ **Directions:** Please check the response that best describes how well you think the following elements of *Unitas* worked. Please write any additional comments in the space provided. If you need more space, use the back of the page. This evaluation is for the presenters, sponsor couples, and parish staff members who participated in this cycle of *Unitas*.

Element	Worked very well	Worked well	Did not work very well	Useless	We didn't use it
Initial Staff Interview with FOCCUS					
Using FOCCUS with a Sponsor Couple					
Separate Beginnings Session					
Enrollment Ritual					
Introductions and Priorities Exercise					
Theology of Marriage					
Principles of Communication					
Negotiation Strategies					
Understanding Self					
Understanding Family of Origin					
Values Discussion					
The Church's Role in Supporting Values					
Conscience Formation					
Celebration of Encouragement					
Sunday Ritual: Prayer for the Couple					
Intimacy					
Church's Teaching on Sexuality					
Practical Issues					
Balancing Career and Family					
Defining Spirituality					
Building Faith in the Home					
Concluding Sunday Liturgy					
Liturgy Planning Session					

1. Please comment on specific things that need improvement. Why do they need to improve?

2. Please make specific suggestions for the things that need improvement.

PART FIVE

AFFIRMATION: MINISTRY TO THE NEWLY MARRIED

CHAPTER 1

Introducing AFFIRMATION

In the RCIA, the *Mystagogia* is the time when the newly baptized, along with the entire community, work to understand the paschal mystery more deeply and to integrate it into their lives more fully.

In *Unitas*, AFFIRMATION functions in the same way. It has two goals:

- To help couples deepen their marriage commitment.
- To help strengthen couples' ties to the parish community.

Studies show that the time following the wedding celebration is critical for the newly married. While many couples may leave the parish, some will undoubtedly stay in the area, and other newly married couples will move into the area. Offering continuing support for these couples is a service to them and highlights the community's commitment to marriage. The AFFIRMATION process simply is a follow–up opportunity for all newly married couples in the community.

AFFIRMATION includes:

- A reflection session to discuss the impact of the wedding celebration on the couple, family, and friends.
- Structured discussion on topics of interest to newly married couples.
- A refresher of some of the skills taught in *Unitas*.
- Social time for newly married couples.

During our development period, we gathered information and ideas about AFFIRMATION from engaged couples and parish staff at St. Peter the Apostle, Islip Terrace, NY; St. Anthony's, Sacramento, CA; and Our Lady of Nazareth, Roanoke, VA. We are grateful for their suggestions, many of which follow.

CHAPTER 2

*Ministry to
the Newly Married*

Beginning AFFIRMATION

Most of the newly married couples with whom we talked believed that AFFIRMATION works best when started about six months after the wedding. They felt that this would give the couples some time to adjust to their new situation.

The couples thought that meeting every month or every other month for the first year of marriage would be very helpful to them. They felt that the group should decide how many times they would meet—some of them have very heavy school or work commitments in the early years of marriage. Above all, they do not want to feel burdened by this.

Some couples move into an area shortly after they are married. Therefore, AFFIRMATION should be open to all young married couples in the parish, whether or not they have participated in *Unitas*. Ideally couples should be at least somewhat involved in the life of the church, and married for no more than three years.

The couples specifically wanted the evenings to be divided among content, couple discussion, and group discussion. They also wanted the evenings to include some social time and some time for prayer.

Some pastoral staff members and married couples asked for reading materials to accompany each session. They felt that couples would benefit from specific articles on a topic. All couples should prepare for every session by completing the reading materials.

Each session should be no more than two hours, and should include ample time for socializing. The session also should be flexible enough to accommodate the needs and wishes of the couples. For example, the couples could discuss the topics for the first hour and a half, and end with social time, or they could discuss for 45 minutes, break for 30 minutes and end with a 45-minute discussion period. Affirmation should be structured—always keeping in mind the wishes of the young married couples.

In the RCIA, the *Mystagogia* calls the newly baptized to reach beyond themselves. We believe that the same thing should happen here. Couples should realize that by building their relationships, they can have an impact on the community. They also affect the community by their presence and their actions. Couples should consider how their values and choices have an impact on others—themselves, family members, and the church community.

Some Practical Tips for the Sessions

1. Every session is informal. Prior to the meeting, couples are given an article or some other discussion starter. This enables the couples to prepare for the discussion topic.

2. At the beginning of each session there is a short period of prayer or biblical reflection. Total discussion time is limited to no more than 90 minutes. (This allows time for socializing.)

3. A couple facilitator is key to the process. One suggestion: the couple facilitator for each session could be someone who has already participated in AFFIRMATION. For the first time you use AFFIRMATION, a married couple from the marriage formation team could take responsibility for each session.

4. At the end of the discussion period, close with shared prayer or another biblical reflection.

5. For the social time, the group can assume responsibility for bringing snacks and beverages.

We believe that as AFFIRMATION develops in a parish, an extended enrichment process for married couples will follow naturally. All married couples need our support.

This section represents a simple outline for an AFFIRMATION group. In 1999, *Unitas* will have a full marriage enrichment program for the early years available. It will be tested at various sites around the country in 1998.

Suggested Topics for a
Six-Session AFFIRMATION Period

Session 1: The Spirituality of the Wedding Day and Early Marriage

First Segment: Wedding Liturgies—The Beginning of Married Life

☞ **Discussion Question:** What impact did your wedding liturgy and wedding reception have on the beginning of your marriage?

Second Segment: "Marriage is a partnership of the whole of life."

☞ **Discussion Question:** What does "partnership" in marriage mean?

Session 2: Communication Skills: Plumbing the Depths

First Segment: Building Listening Skills

☞ **Discussion question:** How well do you listen to each other?

Second Segment: Developing Honesty with Love

☞ **Discussion question:** What happens to a relationship when you stop telling your partner what he or she wants to hear?

Session 3: Values and Choices

First Segment: Values and Choices in Early Marriage

☞ **Discussion Question:** Have any of your choices caused difficulties in your relationship so far?

Second Segment: Application of Values and Choices

☞ **Couple Activity:** Write down every single thing you need to do this week, and explore your weekly calendars together. How much time do you have for each other?

Session 4: Adjustments!—Balancing Relationships with Others

First Segment (30 minutes): Balancing Relationships with Family Members

✍ **Discussion Questions:** How has your family of origin adjusted to your marriage? Have they helped or hindered you? How and why?

Second Segment (30 minutes): Your Life with Friends after Marriage

Discussion Question: How do friends help or hurt your marriage?

Third Segment (30 minutes): Relationships with the Church Community

✍ **Discussion Question:** What role does the local Church community play in our marriage?

Session 5: Finances

First Segment: The Meaning of Money in Marriage

✍ **Discussion Questions:** What does money mean to you? How does that meaning affect your marriage?

Second Segment: Practical Strategies for Financial Management

✍ Use community resources such as accountants and financial planners to help you.

Session 6: Nurturing Intimacy

First Segment: Building Intimacy with Busy Schedules

✍ **Discussion Question:** Has our intimacy grown since we were married?

Second Segment: Practical Strategies for Building Intimacy

✍ **Discussion Question:** What are some concrete suggestions for nurturing intimacy in your relationship?

Follow-Through

St. Anthony's Parish in Sacramento, CA, has evolved a wonderful support community for the married couples in their parish. The group offers service to the parish and wider community, schedules social events for couples and families, and meets once a month for support and prayer. They offer this as marriage enrichment to all their couples.

Here is the text of a letter the Married Couples of St. Anthony gave to every engaged couple at the end of *Unitas*.

Dear Engaged Couple,

Congratulations on your completion of Unitas. *The entire faith community at St. Anthony's welcomes you and prays for you as you continue on your journey to the Sacrament of Marriage.*

The Married Couples of St. Anthony especially welcome you to the Parish. We strongly believe your married life will benefit from membership in this group. That is why we are making each couple who participated in Unitas *automatic members for the 1997–1998 year. We encourage you to renew your membership for 1998–1999. That membership drive will take place in the fall of 1998.*

We have enclosed for you informational literature on the Married Couples of St. Anthony. One of your members stated at the session on "Spirituality of Marriage:" "One way we can contribute our talents to the faith community is to participate in parish events that enrich and support other parishioners in the Christian values of marriage and family life." That is the precise philosophy of the Married Couples of St. Anthony.

We have made a personal appeal to every member of the Married Couples of St. Anthony to be present at your concluding celebration mass this Saturday evening. Our members will be present in force to pray for you and to congratulate you.

We look forward to seeing you at upcoming events this year and the years to come.

Welcome!

No matter what sort of structured program or informal group you decide on, we believe that you must provide support for newly married couples in your community. We believe that newly married ministry will be invaluable not only for the newly married couples but for the entire community. We have no doubt that you will reap the benefits of couples who stay connected to the parish long after their weddings. Even if some couples leave your area, others will come to take their place and find welcome and support for their marriages in your community. Newly married ministry is a long-term investment in the future of your community.